The Story of the
MOTORCYCLE

The Story of the
MOTORCYCLE
Don Morley

Photographic acknowledgments
Eric Kitchen: page 112. Adrian Morris: page 39. National Motor Museum:
pages 10 top, 12 (all three), 13, 16-17, 32-33, 37, 40 top, 46-47.
Nick Nicholls: pages 30-31, 57, 76 top, 86, 96.
All other photographs by Don Morley

Front cover: Honda C.B.X.550 (Don Morley).
Back cover: Honda and Kawasaki (Don Morley).
Endpapers: Yamaha sidecar (Don Morley).
Title page: Freddie Spencer (U.S.A.) on a Honda (Don Morley).

**This edition produced exclusively for
W H Smith**

Published by
Dean's International Publishing
A division of The Hamlyn Publishing Group Limited
London · New York · Sydney · Toronto
Astronaut House, Feltham, Middlesex, England

Copyright © The Hamlyn Publishing Group Limited 1983
ISBN 0 603 03116 1

Printed and bound by Graficromo s.a., Cordoba, Spain

Contents

The Veteran Age

With the birth of the internal-combustion engine in the late 19th century, fathered by such pioneer inventors as Nikolaus August Otto and Gottlieb Daimler, came the inevitable prediction that this creation would one day supply the power to transport the masses. It was somewhat harder, however, to foresee the manner in which the engine would be used, adapted and developed.

Even those men of genius were, in a sense, hamstrung by what went before: horses and carts, stage coaches and the recently introduced pedal cycle. Sheer logic and commonsense led early pioneers simply to remove the horse or the pedaller. It was not realized until many years later that those very vehicles so suitable for the horse might *not*, in fact, be suitable for the internal-combustion engine.

By 1897 numerous inventors, mainly in Germany and France, produced internal-combustion engines in sufficiently large enough numbers to supply the home market and to export abroad. These engines were sold to cycle manufacturers who virtually clipped them on to existing – and incidentally still primitive – pedal-powered bicycles or tricycles, such as Raleigh, Ariel, Werner, the American Orient, Matchless, Bradbury, Rover and Peugeot.

Pre-market development had been almost nil in the initial rush to cash in on public demand for such incredible new novelties. Unfortunately engineering skills and design knowledge were also dangerously limited, aided and abetted by the total ignorance of metallurgic stresses and strains that those early machines would soon face driven by unskilled hands on unsurfaced roads. It is hardly surprising then that so many of the powered cycles built before 1910 were little more than unreliable toys, or that so many of their designers were forced into premature bankruptcy as their untested products failed in public hands.

Frenchman Maurice Fournier displays his sophisticated 1903 V4 'Clement' racer. He was competing in the 1904 Gordon Bennett race held in France.

One of the world's oldest surviving motorcycles still running today, this is an 1898 Holden.

At the risk of offending the veteran purist or collector, these were not, and are not, considered classic motorcycles, though fortunately they are justifiably saved, collected, honoured and displayed at museums, offering later generations a chance to inspect and marvel at such pieces of living history.

Some machines, however, such as the American-built Indian, and Alfred Scott's famous two-speed two stroke, which had all-chain drive and brilliant original designs as far back as 1911, shone out like beacons many years ahead of their time.

It is the intention of the author, therefore, to recall throughout these pages those machines that found fame as the industry's innovating milestones. Some were quite simply good and produced in vast numbers, while others were exceptional at achieving the purpose for which they were intended. Most of these machines are even usable today.

As the momentum gathered in that early quest for a reliable motorcycle, the years 1901 to 1903 were perhaps the most productive and innovative. The new and immature industry had learned many lessons from each other's failings and these lessons bore fruit throughout that period. An increasingly regular supply of relatively proven and reliable engines flooded out of their respective factories.

The French De Dion and Minerva Companies, Germany's Hilldebrand and Wolfmüller, Belgium's Sarolea and the Swiss Zedel concerns were amongst the first both to supply engines and then also to construct and sell the complete motorized cycle.

Meanwhile in the United States, inventor Oscar Hedstrom created the 'Indian' marque, while in England the Collier brothers opened their Matchless factory, though using foreign brought-in engines, and Alfred Scott patented his first revolutionary two-stroke.

By the end of 1903 many of those early motorcycle manufacturers had begun to build and improve their or their suppliers' engines, usually under licence from their original inventors, and some had taken the first faltering steps towards an entirely in-house design and towards machines that were no longer simply powered pedal cycles.

In 1903 the Belgian company, F.N. (today more famous for its NATO armaments), took what was perhaps the greatest giant step forward in the field of motorcycling, a step unmatched until the 1980s. In 1903 the company introduced its virtually mass-produced, four-cylinder, shaft-driven, 'designed-as-an-entity' motorcycle.

Though still obviously imperfect, the F.N. was staggeringly ahead of its time. When all others were totally reliant for their forward transmission on crude leather-thonged and often near-lethal belt drives which universally slipped, slithered or broke, yesterday's F.N. had exactly the same final transmission as today's car or superbike.

However, while two cylinders were relatively common so soon after the turn of the century, four cylinders most certainly were not, a situation that continued despite the efforts of such companies as the American Henderson concern and the British front-runners, Brough

The F.N.'s tank motif displays that company's primary business then as now.

Right: The F.N., designed and built in Belgium, had four cylinders and shaft drive from 1903, though pedals were still fitted. This 1911 model has had the pedals removed.

8

One hero actually competed in his shirt-sleeves.

Left : A typical turn-of-the-century motorcycling cartoon.

Below : Note the resemblance between these motorcycles and an ordinary pedal cycle in this early Edwardian impromptu gathering.

and Wilkinson (now, incidentally, more famous for razors), until Japan's Honda invasion of the 1970s. The veteran four-cylinder F.N. was produced in 496-cc or 748-cc form right through until 1924 with little change. So far was it ahead of its time that its eventual demise came not because it was by then dated, but simply that it had become too expensive to produce.

In its original form, the F.N. employed a car-type in-line four-cylinder side-valve engine with self-acting (atmospheric) inlet valves and a forward-mounted car-type magneto, thus offering a specification years ahead of its opposition. By 1911 this machine had also added a modern-type car clutch along with a rather primitive two-speed gearbox which, unusually, was part of the actual shaft drive. Placed alongside the rear wheel, it acted rather like a crude version of the modern lathe gearbox, with a neutral or non-drive position. The front fork was equally advanced and not unlike the double leg (parallelogram) unit fitted later. Perhaps it may even have been copied by the American Harley-Davidson concern, whose own fork was also to be made later under licence in England by George Brough under the 'Castle' trade-mark. It gave a degree of comfort and steering precision coupled to first rate handling previously undreamed of on any machine.

Meanwhile, in 1890s England, Alfred Scott of Bradford was happily involved in serving an apprenticeship as an engineer involved in marine steam engines. The lessons learned were to serve him in good stead a mere few years later when his mind turned to the internal-combustion engine. Scott's interest lay in the two-stroke engine, and indeed his patents and designs have withstood the passage of time; they are still in use in the latest Grand Prix racing motorcycles. However, his main concern in 1897 was as an inventor rather than a manufacturer.

Scott's first machine was a single-cylinder two-stroke engine which he literally bolted on to a pedal cycle – no more than an experiment. From this, however, the Bradford engineer took out a number of patents leading both to the first practical two-stroke engine, and also to the first practical parallel twin.

Scott was truly a man of genius whose inventions were more than just brilliant. His unique engineering skill and understanding of metal stresses had enabled him, by 1908, to design and build an all-chain-driven two-cylinder and two-speed two-stroke motorcycle, with almost-modern telescopic front-fork damping, and even a kick starter. More importantly, his machine was designed as a complete entity and did not even incorporate pedals, for he was rightly confident that his engine was so powerful that such impedimenta were unnecessary. Furthermore his motorcycle frame bore little or no resemblance to a

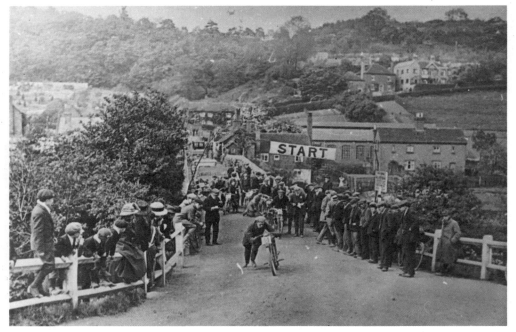

Above right : Years ahead of its time, this oldest known surviving twin-cylinder two-stroke Scott, built in 1910, had all-chain drive, two speeds, teleforks and an engine capacity of 450 cc or ½ horsepower.

Hillclimbing was a popular sport during the early 20th century and drew large crowds to see the combatants test themselves and their machines as they raced against the clock.

This beautiful old picture truly captures the spirit of the hillclimb in which such machines as the Scott made their name.

Scott's unique two-speed drive was not a gearbox but two entirely separate drive-chain ratios, each of which could be coupled or uncoupled via a heel- and toe-operated foot pedal. Neutral or non-drive was in the middle and even a kick starter was fitted.

pushbike; it was a straight-tube diamond-pattern bridge-type structure. He had even taken out patents to allow for water cooling, though oddly enough, his early machines were not so fitted. Initially Scott had no plans to build or market his own designs, and so these early two-strokes which carried his name were built by the Jowett Motorcar Company on his behalf.

In his quest for further knowledge and development, Scott decided to enter his own machine, to be ridden by himself, in the then-popular sport of hillclimbing. Here his two-stroke caused something of a sensation. It is well recorded that as the other competitors pushed and shoved, ran and bumped, trying to coax their somewhat crude machines into life in order to begin these contests, let alone get to the top of the hills, Scott merely sat on his machine with his engine still and silent, quite unconcerned about the others' misfortunes. Only when his turn to compete came, did he gently press the rather delicate kick starter to bring his engine purring to life while still astride his machine. He proceeded to demoralize all opposition by winning four consecutive gold medals as he smashed the speed records in the unlimited capacity, twin-cylinder and variable-gear classes, leaving every other manufacturer or rider aghast.

After frantic behind-the-scenes meetings, Scott's opponents persuaded the governing body of the sport in Great Britain, the Autocycle Union, that the Jowett Scott was illegal. They claimed that it was, after all, a two-stroke and as such its engine fired every other stroke which, remembering that it was a twin, meant in real terms an explosion every stroke, whereas they, the opposition, all built four-stroke engines. It was, they claimed, grossly unfair to allow such an engine and machine, like the distinctly delicate and lightweight Scott with its cylinders firing and therefore propelling it more often than theirs, to be allowed to compete. Fortunately, rather than a total ban the governing body announced instead that in future any Scott machine would be handicapped.

*Below: Frank Philipp poses on his
500-cc Scott after competing in the
1911 Senior T.T.*

*Above right: The irrepressible Freddie
Dixon on his Brooklands racing Vee-
twin American Harley-Davidson.*

Far from being disappointed or annoyed, the shrewd businessman
Scott was in fact jubilant on hearing this decision. He answered his
critics with a brilliant advertising campaign, 'The machine all others are
afraid of'. The resulting publicity brought instant public demand for
these purring, or rather yowling, two-strokes and ironically forced Scott
at last to become a manufacturer in 1909, to increase production where
Jowett could not, and meet these new demands.

By 1911 the two speeder had yet again been entered in the Isle of Man
T.T. (Tourist Trophy) Races, this time to be held over the new 37·75-
mile mountain course which is still used today. Scott's machines were to
be ridden by his brother-in-law and fellow Company Director, Frank
Philipp, along with Eric Myers and Frank Applebee, against perhaps
the third most significant machine of the era, the American built and
designed 'Indian', which actually won the race. Frank Philipp's Scott
did at least shatter the lap record before breaking down. (Incidentally,

the three 1911 works Scotts used a rotary induction valve of the type finally rediscovered by the Japanese as recently as 1979, when American ace Kenny Roberts' World-Championship-winning Yamaha was so fitted.)

Turning the T.T. tables in both 1912 and 1913 races, Scotts romped home the winners and continued to smash lap records again in 1914. But it was in trials that this particular marque will perhaps be best remembered in 1914. Apart from winning a Gold Medal in the Autocycle Union's Six Days Reliability Trial, Alfred Scott and his employees devised what was and still is the toughest motorcycle trial in the world.

The 1914 Scott Trial route was 90 miles along. Of one river crossing the magazine *Motorcycle*'s correspondent reported that 'Every competitor was forced to a halt with the whole of his engine, magneto and carburettor under water'. Yet still the machines were re-started and went on to finish the distance.

This 1920s racing Indian as used by F. W. (Freddie) Dixon and H. (Bert) Le Vack was a highly successful T.T. machine, with its all-chain drive, twin-cylinder torque and twistgrip-controlled throttle.

13

This is the actual T.T. Matchless as ridden by manufacturer Charlie Collier in the 1913 T.T. He used a similar machine in his grudge race against Jake de Rosier's American Indian.

Despite the fact that this event was, from the outset, thrown open to all other makes, Scott two-speed machines won every single Scott Trial between 1914 and 1924. This 'monopoly' further demoralized the opposition and confirmed the superiority of the model's virtually unchanged design which (in both 500-cc and 600-cc form) lasted right through until the 1930s.

It is a considerable tribute to Alfred Scott's undoubted genius that his 1908 two-speed motorcycle is hardly discernable from the final production versions made over 20 years later, long after Scott himself had left the very company he founded. In 1919 he turned to pastures new, before dying at the early age of 48 from the ill effects of pneumonia contracted during a pot-holing expedition.

His living memorial is that more machines were built in his name and to his designs and patents after his death than in his own lifetime, and that many of even the pre-1919 machines are still perfectly capable of being ridden and coping well with today's modern traffic conditions.

Meanwhile, in the United States of America in 1901, the 'Hendee', later to be renamed the 'Indian', had commenced production, soon to be

Overleaf : Perhaps the most famous veteran road-racing machine of all, Pa Norton's 'Old Miracle' 500-cc sidevalve model first raced in 1912.

followed by the equally legendary Harley-Davidson concern, which survives to today. Like Scotts, the Indian company had dispensed with pedal-cycle tradition and thus also became the forerunners of the true motorcycle.

The American company produced both single- and twin-cylinder engined machines. The singles design was unique in that it was not only half of the twin, but that the remaining cylinder sloped backwards, unlike any other machine.

Lee Evans entered a twin-cylinder Indian model in the 1907 T.T. and only just narrowly missed beating Britain's winner, Harry Collier, who had ridden his self-built Matchless. But a mere four years later the Indian factory again returned, not just to win, but to take the first three places in the twin-cylinder races, suitably aided by their two-speed gearboxes and all-chain drive which, along with Scotts, placed them in a development class of their own.

During the 1911 T.T. arch-rivals, Jake de Rosier (Indian) and Charlie Collier (Matchless), were both disqualified for technical offences, leaving the questions of their personal abilities and machines'

much-argued-over merits undecided, and resulting in what was to become a historic challenge.

As a decider the Brooklands race track near London was to become the venue in 1911 for the first trans-Atlantic Match Race, where Collier and de Rosier entered three races against each other to decide who was superior.

De Rosier and his Indian won to establish himself and the American T.T. winning marque as the finest road-racing machine of the time and so, incidentally, considerably increasing the American machine's popularity and reputation.

Not only did the single- and twin-cylinder Indian models justifiably claim to be the most advanced motorcycles ever, but they also became the leading imported machine throughout Europe, going on to be by far the most successful sidecar power in military use throughout the First World War.

Now one of the world's rarest machines, this Edmund is that company's 1914 spring-frame model. The entire saddle, petrol tank and footboard assembly are suspended on the rather large multi-leaf springs which can be seen behind the saddle.

The original backwards-leaning single or Vee-twins from this Springfield, Massachusetts company also introduced another world first: there was not a single throttle or brake cable to be seen, for Indian engineer Oscar Hedstrom and Founder George M. Hendee liked their products to look tidy. These machines relied instead on beautifully engineered and hidden steel rod controls, that ran via knuckle joints right inside and through the actual handlebars and frame, forming a unique though costly control system (which also, incidentally, included the world's first twist grip throttle control that has become universally accepted on every modern machine).

Despite such innovations and racing successes as recorded by those famous Indians (including in 1911 the very first foreign T.T. win as well as the very first T.T. 1-2-3), the U.S.'s other early giants such as Harley-Davidson, Excelsior and Flying Merkel had begun to close the development gap.

Overleaf: This 1914 N.U.T. (Newcastle upon Tyne) is the actual T.T. model with its famous 90-bore 1000-cc Vee-twin J.A.P. engine that was to dominate track racing for many years.

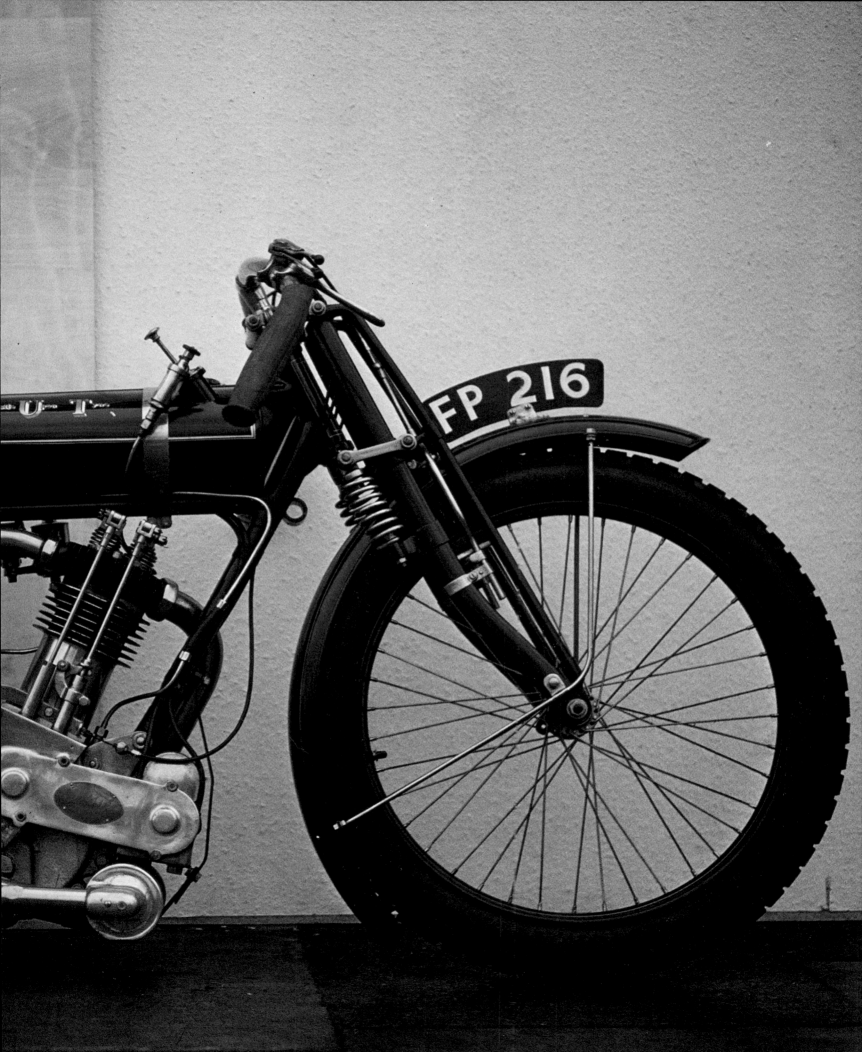

However, when peace resumed after the First World War, instead of continuing to lead the world, the American competitors floundered in an era defined by the cheap Ford 'T' motorcar. The industry stagnated for many years, producing merely soft, docile and stodgy means of transport, far removed from the rest of the world's great race tracks.

Ironically if the First World War finished American international sporting achievements, it made, or at least laid the foundations, for the successes of the Bristol firm of Douglas, whose horizontally opposed flat-twin motorcycles were developed from Joseph Barter's 'Fee' machine which had commenced Douglas production as the Model 'A' in 1907.

The Model 'A', like its Fee predecessor, was perhaps the perfect *bad* example of cheaply clipping an engine, albeit a very good engine, onto an ordinary standard pushbike, suggesting little of either the design eminence or sporting achievements that were to come. Even by 1909 the 'Dougies', as these machines affectionately became known, were seemingly light years behind Scott or Indian. It took until the Model 'D' (or 1910) before a significant improvement became apparent. The most noticeable difference was the lowering of the engine height in the frame. It was the 1912 2¾-horsepower Model 'G' that really pointed the way for the future. Although it still had pedals and belt drive, this machine sold in vast numbers, and led to further models right through to the open framed ladies' model ('X') in 1914.

It was the 2¾ Douglas that almost singlehandedly put motorcycling on the man-in-the-street's map. Douglas had supplied by far the most machines to the British Expeditionary Forces during the First World War, and on these vehicles a whole generation learned to ride both off-road and on.

Left: The immortal 2¾-horsepower 1914 Douglas, examples of which went to war in their thousands. Though belt-driven and relatively primitive, these ultra-lightweight flat twins transported a military generation.

Seventy years on, this veteran Triumph tackles the sort of going that it may once have encountered on the Flanders battlefields in 1914.

Seen here in its home environment, in the paddock of the Laguna Seca Raceway in California, this 1919 American Harley-Davidson C.A. Series '61' twin is still actively vintage racing.

The 2¾ was basically a crude, even dated, simple lightweight chassis into which paradoxically an advanced and highly efficient flat twin engine had been fitted. The whole ensemble was so light that it could – and often had to be – picked up and carried, and despite its primitive belt drive, the Dougie endeared itself to a generation of despatch riders.

Over 20,000 2¾ Douglases went to war, many to be returned from the Somme when peace returned. These formed the backbone of the cheap 'transport for the people' era. Indeed, that very same W.D. model continued in production in peacetime colours right through until 1920. It is little wonder that more of these machines are still running today than any other veterans. Belt-driven and often clutchless right up until 1922, the Douglas models, by most rules, should not even be considered for the accolade 'Classic', yet their very lightness and silky smooth understressed horizontally opposed side-valve engines, rendered more modern ancillaries virtually unnecessary. The rider merely sat astride, paddled off with his feet, and usually before half a stride had been taken, his docile mount was happily chuffing away untemperamentally under its own steam.

In a mere 14 years from the turn of the century the motorcycle had progressed from the unreliable and difficult-to-handle clip-on engine to the relatively sophisticated machine that fought a war, provided transport for millions and became the ready steed for the new sports of trials riding and road racing.

The Roaring Twenties

Post First World War motorcycles outwardly continued much as before, though the pushbike-type pedals had all but disappeared. Most were still belt-driven with inadequate cycle-type stirrup brakes that could not even begin to slow down these already-speeding monsters. Stopping on roads that were still relatively void of traffic was considered of little consequence compared with the quest to make the machines travel faster and faster.

Inwardly, however, designs were becoming far more modern, with gearboxes and clutches to smooth the take-off and power delivery, better magnetos, carburettors, ignition and lighting systems, and perhaps most important for human comfort, with saddles designed for the purpose rather than borrowed from either pushbike or horse.

A beautiful example of a racing Sunbeam 90 photographed by the roadside in the Isle of Man, where it was still in use during 1982.

Chain drives were becoming more common as the 'peaceful' 1920s began with its readymade market of war-trained riders. The public clamoured for motorcycles, often for sidecars too with which to transport themselves and family to work and play, but the veteran-looking flat-tank style still reigned supreme.

As Europe entered the International Grand Prix era, it drew further away from its American counterparts. In the U.S.A. the Milwaukee Harley-Davidson side valvers ('flat heads') assumed Indians' sporting mantle, and the rest of the world began its search for even greater performance via overhead pushrod-operated valves.

George Dance, the famous Sunbeam star, had made his own O.H.V. conversion for Sunbeam's long-stroke 3½ horsepower (500 cc) and had become unbeatable over Europe's sprint races and hillclimbs. Sunbeam itself, along with many others of the day's sporting companies, was soon to copy and follow Dance's lead.

The Sunbeam motorcycles constructed by John Marsden were quality built in England's Midland Black Country, and so, naturally, were never enamelled in any colour other than deep black gloss, set off with gold lining and nickel plating, to further embellish the quality machines.

Though this marque had contested the 1914 T.T. with a creditable joint second place in the Senior Race, it was the first post-war T.T. in 1920 that really put Sunbeam on the racing map, when Tommy De La Hay won the Senior Race at an average speed of 51·48 mph.

On similar machines, W. R. Brown was third and George Dance smashed all records with a 55·62 mph lap before retiring with engine problems. Incredibly these 90+ mph T.T. machines were not only still flat tankers but relied on the ludicrously inadequate, for such speeds, belt rim brakes. They hardly cried out 'innovation'.

Sunbeam did, however, break new ground by using an aluminium alloy piston, overhead valves set at 45 degrees, and a modern style central sparking plug position, to sire the famous 'Sunbeam 90' which has become such a collector's item today.

Above : Designed and built by William 'Bill' Henderson in Philadelphia, this 1168-cc ACE machine had four cylinders and a car-type gearbox in 1920.

Left : A beautiful period cartoon.

BALLIG BRIDGE—the most spectacular point on the Isle of Man course.

Countless Grand Prix successes, Scottish Six Day Trial Awards, and three T.T. wins later, by 1929, the works machines had tried and then abandoned an overhead cam engine design and had adopted drum brakes and saddle-type petrol tanks, to otherwise end the decade as it began with another, but this time unsuccessful, works T.T. challenge.

Replicas of the works racers were sold to the public in the form of the Supertuned '90' model, and later even the '95' (the 'numbers' signifying the sort of speeds their owners could expect them to attain) but unfortunately, despite the Sunbeam's undoubtedly fine engineering, the factory, like the 'Indians' before them, had already stayed too long with a dated design.

Sunbeams were sold off in the 1930s to Associated Motorcycles, who already owned A.J.S. and Matchless, then sold again to B.S.A. with little more than a shadow of their former glory and then finally were allowed to die away with token dignity.

Quite delectable, this 1920 touring model Indian 'Scout' Vee-twin with its matching period sidecar.

Famous 1920s track racer Nigel Spring and his erstwhile passenger seem taken aback by the fact that their Brooklands racing Norton has thrown off its sidecar wheel and so crashed.

Meanwhile, Triumph, who like Douglas had supplied many machines to the Allied armies during the 1914-18 Holocaust, had also resumed peacetime production with much the same tired, already old-fashioned bread-and-butter mounts. Unusual for the era, Triumph looked outside of its own factory and design team and engaged the famous engineer, Sir Harry Riccardo, to invent the superbike of the 1920s. Unfortunately, Riccardo's undoubtedly brilliant original design was so watered down when it reached the actual production machines that much of the impetus was lost.

Riccardo had invented an all-new single-cylinder engine with a radical four-valve cylinder head and valve timing. The experimental model proved to be an instant flyer and eminent racing mount, but Triumph instead chose to cheapen the design and compromise. Basically the production version of the 'Riccy', as it became known, had a simpler and appreciably less efficient overhead four-valve arrangement than its inventor had envisaged, and was merely grafted onto one of Triumph's existing old-fashioned engines to save production costs.

Though loved by a generation after its 1921 introduction, the Riccardo was really a story of what might have been: Rudge and later Honda ruled the world's road and race tracks with the designs and in the manner that Riccardo had first intended for Triumph.

When one door closes, another invariably opens. As the various established 1920s manufacturers' fortunes waxed or waned, such makes as Rudge, Velocette, A.J.S., Rex Acme, Levis, Cotton, New Imperial,

New Gerrard, Dot, H.R.D., and Norton all vied for racing successes and the resulting publicity and sales. Some initiated rivalries that would last for decades; others failed and disappeared almost overnight during the Great Depression.

A.J.S. had long been both a successful manufacturer and racing factory when the 1920s dawned, and indeed kicked off that decade with a 1920 Junior T.T. win with a delightful little overhead-valve 350 cc, that was to sell like hot cakes in roadster form. The win was, in reality, a near thing for the Wolverhampton-based A.J.S. team, for of the eight machines entered for the race, six had retired and even the winner, Eric Williams, broke down over a mile from the finish. Fortunately, he was so far ahead of the opposition that he still had time to push his bike home to win.

Most of the A.J.S. problems during that race lay in the fact that its design was really too advanced for the technology of the day, with such forward-thinking ideas as a six-speed gearbox, all-chain drive, 1980s-

Below left : One of the most famous rider-tuners of all during the 1920s and 1930s, Bill Lacey demonstrates the riding position of the Grindlay-Peerless on which he broke the World Speed Record.

Above : Lacey in record-breaking action showing his windcheating style on the Brooklands banked track.

style pent-roof cylinder combustion chamber, and an over 75 mph performance for a 350 cc. So much faster were these machines than those of their rivals that the Stephens Brothers were not only able to de-tune them to increase reliability for the following year, but also reduce the number of gears to a simpler and more manageable three speeds. These ploys paid off when A.J.S. took the first three places in the 1921 Junior T.T. More incredibly, and never repeated, the de-tuned 350-cc version in the hands of H. R. Davies went on to win the 500-cc race, despite its obvious capacity handicap, and so made history in being the only Junior motorcycle ever to win the Senior T.T. let alone break the bigger class's overall race record at 54·50 mph. With internal expanding brakes, all-chain drive and such a potent engine coupled to an exhaust pipe of massive diameter, the 'Big Ports', as these machines

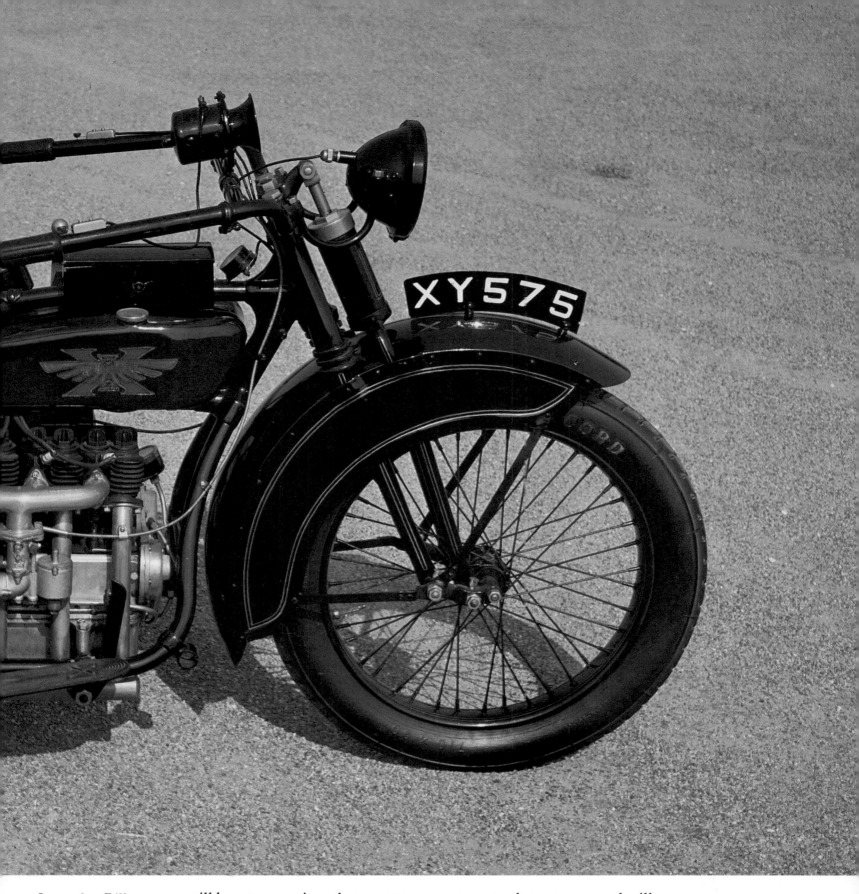

Long after Bill Henderson had sold his design to the Chicago-based Schwinn Company these machines still carried his name. This 1924 1301-cc four-cylinder model was built two years after Henderson died.

are still known, continued to race to many more such successes and will still out-accelerate many similar-capacity machines in use today.

Norton, who had won the twin-cylinder class of the very first T.T. in 1907, had, meanwhile, continued to place its faith in the old side-valve design, and indeed had been particularly successful both in market and track racing terms following its successes at such circuits as Brooklands. But further T.T. successes had eluded the firm. It is claimed that the famous side-valve 16H which was marketed by the Bracebridge Street, Birmingham company continuously from 1912 until the mid-1960s, and which, at one time, formed the very basis of Norton's successful racing efforts, was in fact very nearly a failure.

The tuned racing version known as the Brooklands Special was so named because the factory guaranteed that each engine had been tested and timed at the Brooklands race track in the hands of its then-factory-rider, D. R. O'Donovan, at over 75 mph for a distance of at least one kilometre before being issued with a certificate to that effect. What the factory did not let out was that when it had first so tuned these engines they, embarrassingly, were found to be slower than their production counterparts, a fact which caused frantic inquests at the factory and much work before the reasons were discovered. So little was really known about race tuning in those days that Norton had failed to realize that in polishing the cylinder head and valve areas, the company had in fact reduced the very rough edge gas turbulence that had given so much performance in the first place. Neither did the firm inform the paying public that those Brooklands kilometre speeds were achieved by swooping the machines right up Brooklands giant banking after a long, fast run-up, and then taking those timings as O'Donovan swooped back down again, considerably assisted by the almost 1 in 1 slope.

Not intending to detract from Norton's early performances, these stories are merely anecdotes in the history of this great factory, who, prior to 1922, raced side valves before at last building an overhead-valve 500-cc engine that was to go on to become well-nigh unbeatable in solo

Above: A.J.S.'s famous 350-cc 'Big Port' racer, which created history when piloted by Howard R. Davies in the 1921 T.T. It won the 500-cc race.

Above, far left: Ugly in the extreme, the 1928 four-cylinder 985-cc water-cooled A.J.W. was an attempt to win custom by means of exotica in slumping world markets. Needless to say, it failed.

Left: Sidecar or chariot racing as it used to be called, with the unfortunate passenger just lying prone, unable to see even impending disaster. Here Les Archer (New Imperial) is in the lead from Ben Bickell (Chater-Lea) at Brooklands.

or sidecar form, and in almost every type of motorcycle competition.

The Model 18, as the overhead-valve version was known, still featured the old-fashioned flat tank and was decidedly primitive for its power output. Yet in one year in the hands of Alec Bennett it knocked almost 6 mph off the Isle of Man Senior T.T. Race speed and also won the 1924 sidecar race.

By 1926 the legendary Ulstermen, Stanley Woods and Joe Craig, the latter eventually to become Norton's Race Team Manager and tuning wizard, had formed what was perhaps the most powerful racing team ever assembled and by 1927 the overhead-cam racing C.S.1. had itself arrived to win both the Senior T.T. and the Manx Grand Prix.

Designed by Walter Moore, who later became the Chief Designer with the German N.S.U. Company, the C.S.1 was little more than a Model 18 engine and cycle onto which the single overhead-cam drive mechanism was grafted where the pushrods had previously been. It was not merely a fast motorcycle, and certainly never a high revver. Instead, it achieved its speed by sheer power. These big Norton singles, in roadster form, were reckoned to fire just once every lamp post yet still top 100 mph on what seemed little more than engine tick-over speed, and they were reckoned to outhandle virtually any other machine on road or track. Perhaps it was the latter which was the real reason for Norton's success.

John Pugh, Rudge's designer, decided that with this machine the time was ripe to re-enter the racing fray, a decision that very nearly won Rudge the 1928 Senior T.T.; his jockey, Graham Walker, had the race in the bag with over three minutes' lead and less than ten miles to go, when the engine unfortunately failed.

Later that year at the Ulster Grand Prix, neither the factory or Walker made a single mistake as they won at a record speed of over 80 mph, incidentally the first time that any race had ever been won at such a speed. Thus it was not unnatural that when the public road vehicle was announced, it became known as the 'Ulster' model.

Though most of the firm's successes were still to come, these late 1920s Rudges had at least achieved what Riccardo, or rather Triumph, had failed to do with its advanced, though still pushrod-driven, four-valve design, which was greatly aided by large (for the era) coupled brakes to help the machine stop.

Rudge also pioneered the use of chromium instead of nickel-plating for the bright parts on its machines, another first that has lasted until today. The catalogue of Rudge's products, including the 'Ulster' in 1929, stated of its engine:

A.J.S.'s first overhead-camshaft racer, the 1929 350-cc R7 model, with Bert Denly on board.

'*The Ulster Engine*: Pursuing our policy of making our sports engine almost an exact replica of the power units used in the previous year's racing, the 1929 Rudge-Whitworth "Ulster" engine has the deeply ribbed crankcase with both ball and roller bearings on the drive side and a single roller bearing on the timing side which was used on our 1928 T.T. machines.'

'With the exception that still further improvements have been effected in the cylinder head, and by enclosing the valve gear, the rest of the engine, flywheels, big end, connecting rod, pistons, cylinders and lubrication system, with an oil feed to the back of the cylinder, is identical with the racing engines which have gained so many laurels in 1928.'

Before the decade ended, there were both 250-cc and 350-cc versions, the latter in works form even had a five-speed gearbox, an advance for which the owners of roadster machines of any other make, had to wait almost 40 years.

The 1920s had begun with crude beaded-edge tyres, cycle-type brakes, side-valve engines, inadequate total-loss drip-feed lubrication and the old-fashioned slab petrol tanks, hung under a pedal-cycle frame. Competitive test racing led, by the end of the decade, to modern wired-on tyres, expanding drum and (in Douglas's case) disc brakes, positive oil feeds, decent frames and forks and even overhead-cam engines, along with the first of the modern style petrol tanks. The 1920s alone almost bridged the gap between the veterans and the 1980s.

The Sporting Thirties

As 1929 came to a close, almost every manufacturer of large capacity machines listed an O.H.V. or even an overhead-cam model as flagship of the range, and chain drive and expanding brakes had at last become permanent fixtures.

Flat slab tanks had rapidly been replaced by the softer curves of the saddle tank, though the frame itself probably had not been altered. The technique of soft-nickel-plating such items as handlebars, petrol tanks and nuts and bolts had been replaced by the harder and more durable chromium-plating, and modern battery/dynamo electric lighting was at last on the scene if only as an optional extra to banish the primitive and explosive veteran acetylene lamps.

In a nutshell, the modern motorcycle had arrived, along with a profusion of demanding buyers. Yet, ominously, 1929 had also seen the Wall Street Stock Market crash and the beginnings of worldwide economic disaster and depression, not least to the motorcycle industry.

Almost overnight in 1930 many of the greatest manufacturing names in motorcycling were to disappear forever as both their company shares and markets quite literally were wiped out as a result of Wall Street's disastrous shock waves. In the United States machines such as the advanced Henderson and Cleveland 4s went under, to leave Indian and Harley to fight over a relatively meagre market. In Europe both A.J.S. and Ariel went bankrupt (although they were later revived under new ownership). These difficult years saw the end of such machines as new Gerrard, new Hudson, N.U.T., Chater Lea, D.O.T., Rex Acme, Grindley Peerless and many others who found out that even their sporting achievements were not enough to save them.

One of the four-valve Rudges (500 cc) which won the 1930 Senior T.T.

Bill Lacey poses by his copper-plated 500-cc Brooklands racing Grindlay-Peerless J.A.P. outside his trackside tuning establishment.

There began an era of both intense technical development and production rationalization. In a desperate quest for a slice of the rapidly diminishing market, each and every motorcycle maker was forced to offer more, and to do so for much less. Even more bankruptcies occurred as even many of these new masterpieces failed to find sufficient numbers of buyers.

Ariel's hoped-for saviour (although its development was later to bankrupt the firm) was the revolutionary Edward-Turner-designed Square Four – not that four-cylinder motorcycles were by then that unusual, but all of Ariel's predecessors had featured in-line engines, and because of this became necessarily physically long which, in turn, forced unfortunate compromises to be made in their matching frame designs. Turner reasoned that by linking two twin-cylinder engines together in a square formation, his engine would shoehorn into a conventional existing motorcycle frame, and if successful, that machine should handle just as well on the road as the single-cylinder version, but with the added benefits of the four-cylinder performance, acceleration and smoothness.

The vehicle was devised in 1928 and first marketed in 1931 as a four-speed 500-cc overhead-cam-engined machine. Turner had almost produced the exact configuration for the Grand Prix machine of today, whose physical size is still so important. Unfortunately, however, whereas today's racers are water-cooled and therefore not dependent on the wind and the rain for cooling those rear cylinders, Turner's Ariel

44

was not. Although re-designed later as a 600 cc and eventually stretched to a full 1000 cc by the new revitalized Ariel company and remaining in production until the late 1950s, this so-near-to-being-a-world-beater machine never really lived down its justified early reputation for uneven engine cooling, a problem which more often than not under hard usage resulted in the rear cylinders running hotter than the front and seizing.

Meanwhile, George Brough at his Nottingham works had devised a different strategy and formula for market success, aimed not at mass production or even the masses, but instead at the richest, whom he reasoned were, even in those troubled times, inflation-proof.

In truth, Brough never mass-produced a motorcycle, neither was he, strictly speaking, a great designer, though he was often an innovator. He relied instead on copying and improving upon the best features of every

Made in Denmark, this 1934 Nimbus was so ahead of its time, with its pressed-steel frame, air-cooled four-in-line engine and shaft drive, that it remained in production more or less unchanged until 1955.

other product, and then putting them together in one superb quality package, with the finest quality paintwork and craftsmanship of the day.

George Brough's father (W. E.) had been a motorcycle manufacturer, building machines bearing his surname since 1902, before George Brough Junior started his own company at the famous Hayden Road, Nottingham premises during the 1920s to build machines around the J. A. Prestwick (J.A.P.) Vee-twin engines.

George Brough was not a shy man nor was he inclined to hide his light under a bushel. Indeed to distinguish his machines from his father's, or for that matter anyone else's, he called his products 'Brough Superiors', and indeed superior they truly were, for money was of little importance to Brough's famous clients, who numbered such as Lawrence of Arabia, Kings and oil millionaires.

Like so many others, Brough had raced his own side-valve J.A.P.-engined machines to some considerable success during the 1920s, to begin this marque's public recognition. But it was the big, immensely powerful, and expensive O.H.V. 1000-cc Vee-twin SS100 models that were to earn him recognition as producer of the Rolls Royces of motor-

Overleaf: Edward Turner's infamous 1931 Square Four which failed, because of poor cylinder-cooling, to achieve the potential intended for it by its far-sighted designer.

45

cycles during the 1930s. The story is told that when a pressman had so dubbed George's products, the near-by Derby firm of Rolls Royce had not been amused to hear that Brough was using the accolade and the name and hard-won reputation to advertise his motorcycle products. Not unnaturally, Rolls Royce decided to send an emissary to look over the Brough works and report back; the firm would then be in a position to commence legal action with facts to support its claim. Fortunately at the time of the Rolls Royce man's visit to Nottingham, and unknown to him, Brough and his staff were preparing the actual machines for the forthcoming London Olympia Motorcycle Show. Naturally, therefore, the employees were embellishing these bikes with even more than the usual spit and polish, and paying more than lavish attention to detail, all of which was observed by the Rolls Royce visitor on his unexpected arrival. Thus, far from taking the planned hard line, the Rolls emissary reported back to Derby suitably impressed that Brough did indeed justify using the Rolls Royce name. Not only was the quality truly superb, but also he had noticed that Brough's workers assembled their machines wearing kid gloves, something Rolls itself had not thought of! Little did he know, of course, that those gloves were a one-off exercise used only while working on the all-important show models. However, from that time on as the result of the visitor's impression, George

The magnificent sprung-frame Matchless 1000-cc Vee-twin-engined 1939 Brough Superior, regarded as the Rolls-Royce of motorcycles.

Brough's products were for evermore officially blessed by Rolls Royce, who allowed Brough and Brough only to use the Rolls Royce name in his own advertising.

Norton, who had successfully commenced the decade with its overhead-cam-engined C.S.I racer, had soon found itself overshadowed both on the world's race tracks and the marketplace by the four-valve Rudges. Norton, therefore, commissioned designer Arthur Carroll to collaborate with Norton's ace tuner and race chief, Joe Craig, in the hope – brilliantly fulfilled as it turned out – that they could put matters right.

The re-designed 'Carroll' motor was placed in the old C.S.I. cycle for 1931, and it began an era of racing domination that was only occasion-

Right: J. S. Wright on his 996-cc Zenith J.A.P. lapping Brooklands at 117·19 mph in 1929. This machine was once Brough's greatest racing rival.

ally threatened until the mid-1960s and the advent of the Japanese onslaught. After three years in the racing doldrums, Nortons, in that auspicious year of 1931, not only took the first three places in the Senior T.T. in the triumphant hands of Tim Hunt, Jimmy Guthrie, and Stanley Woods, but won almost every other European Road Race too. Norton had certainly bounced back.

Norton had scored a demoralizing Senior T.T. hat trick over the opposition, and Hunt and Guthrie on the 350-cc versions also took first and second place respectively in the Junior Race to demoralize still further the Rudge efforts. After those defeats Rudge never really recovered or regained to any extent its previous racing prestige in either the Junior or the Senior classes.

The German 500-cc N.S.U. racer developed from Walter Moore's original Norton C.S.I. design.

Christened the 'International Model' (usually referred to by enthusiasts as 'The Inter' for short) after its almost instant worldwide racing and marketing success story, these cammy models soon became available in replica form, both as 350s (International Model 40) or 500s (International Model 30). They continued winning races and enjoyed a production run which lasted until 1958.

Racing had – and has – two simple objectives; first, to develop and improve a product that was basically 'as sold' to the public and second, but perhaps even more important, to provide the living (and therefore advertising) proof of both the machine's and its maker's capabilities to potential buyers.

Ironically, with the exception of the hand-built and expensive International models which were priced beyond the reach of all but a few, Norton's incredible string of track successes during those troubled 1930s and the resultant publicity only served, in a sense, to con the public. For the Bracebridge Street, Birmingham factory in the main continued to market over-engineered, yet dated and inadequately designed, staid and stodgy roadsters that had more in common with farm tractors than pedigree racers. Frankly the colour scheme was about all they had in common with the elite 'Inter'.

Such policies sooner or later would inevitably initiate even that great factory's decline, for even on the race tracks where other makers were closing the technology gap, the International model increasingly suffered from its chassis limitations of over-engineering and excess weight. Worse for Norton, Hitler and Mussolini by the mid-1930s had begun to turn the world recession to their own advantage.

Germany and Italy, both suffering an economic climate of unemployment and falling governments, had been ripe for the intervention of dictators whose solutions for national reflation included the creation of vast armaments factories and armies for the war so soon to be fought.

Still racing in Austria today, this 1930s Rudge Ulster was near to the end of that once famous line.

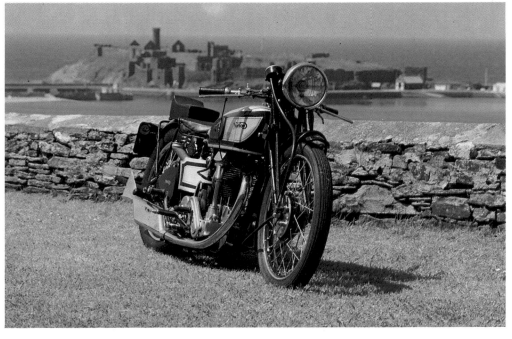

Right : Norton's world-beating pre-war production racer in roadster form, this 1937 350-cc International Model 40 was rebuilt by the author.

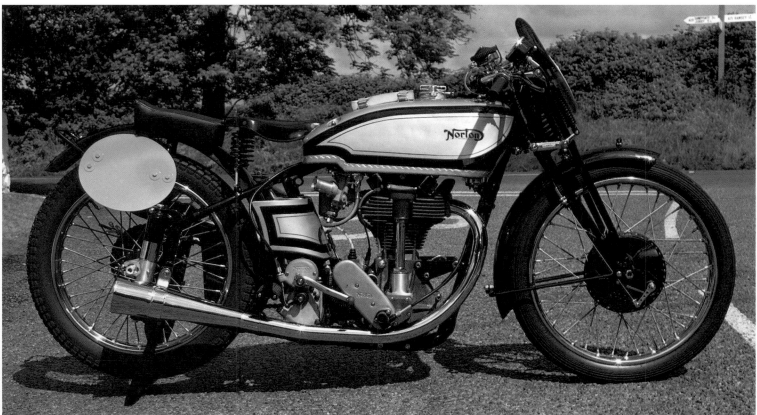

The racer that almost never was, Norton's Manx Grand Prix model, built for the 1939 September races and intended for 1940 production had war not broken out.

It was also necessary and of even more importance than the factories and armies to increase the 'prestige' of both men, to show them as 'winners'.

There was a desire, in fact a *need*, to win all races, whether they be between cars, motorcycles, aeroplanes or people – as witnessed by the infamous 1936 Berlin Olympics. Winning to Italy and Germany at that time meant far more than selling machines when the important prize of national prestige was at stake. Vast sums of government money were made available throughout Germany and Italy to any company prepared to make any racing vehicle, and most especially motorcycles, that would wrest the world speed records from the rest of the world and give them to Germany or Italy.

So aided, Gilera and Moto Guzzi of Italy and D.K.W. and B.M.W. of Germany suddenly found themselves in a position no motorcycle manufacturing company before or since could ever dream of. They had almost unlimited budgets to allow design and material freedom of near

Overleaf: A beautifully restored 1936 Excelsior 350-cc racing Manxman.

Right : The side-valve American Indian that actually won the prestigious Daytona Race in 1938, seen here lapping that famous track once again.

D.K.W. or 'Das Kleine Wunder' ('The Little Wonder') was Hitler's lightweight-class secret racing weapon on the world's late-1930s circuits.

As the war clouds gathered, the immortal Tiger 100, aided by a supercharger, lapped the Brooklands race track at 118·02 mph, while another machine, bored out to 501 cc to qualify it for the 750-cc class, managed 118·06. Unknown to Edward Turner at the time, these records were to stand forever, for within a few short weeks Brooklands had closed to aid the Second World War effort, and was never again re-opened.

An era was over. For seven long years motorcycle production and design once again reverted to the manufacturing of strong durable machines, more suitable to battlefields and mud than race circuits. Equally sadly, many of the individualist manufacturers who had fought and survived the Wall Street Crash, succumbed to forces of the Second World War during the early 1940s.

Overleaf : Edward Turner's immortal 1937 Triumph 500-cc 'Speed Twin', which was to so revolutionize motorcycle design and lives on in Triumph's 'Bonneville' derivative today.

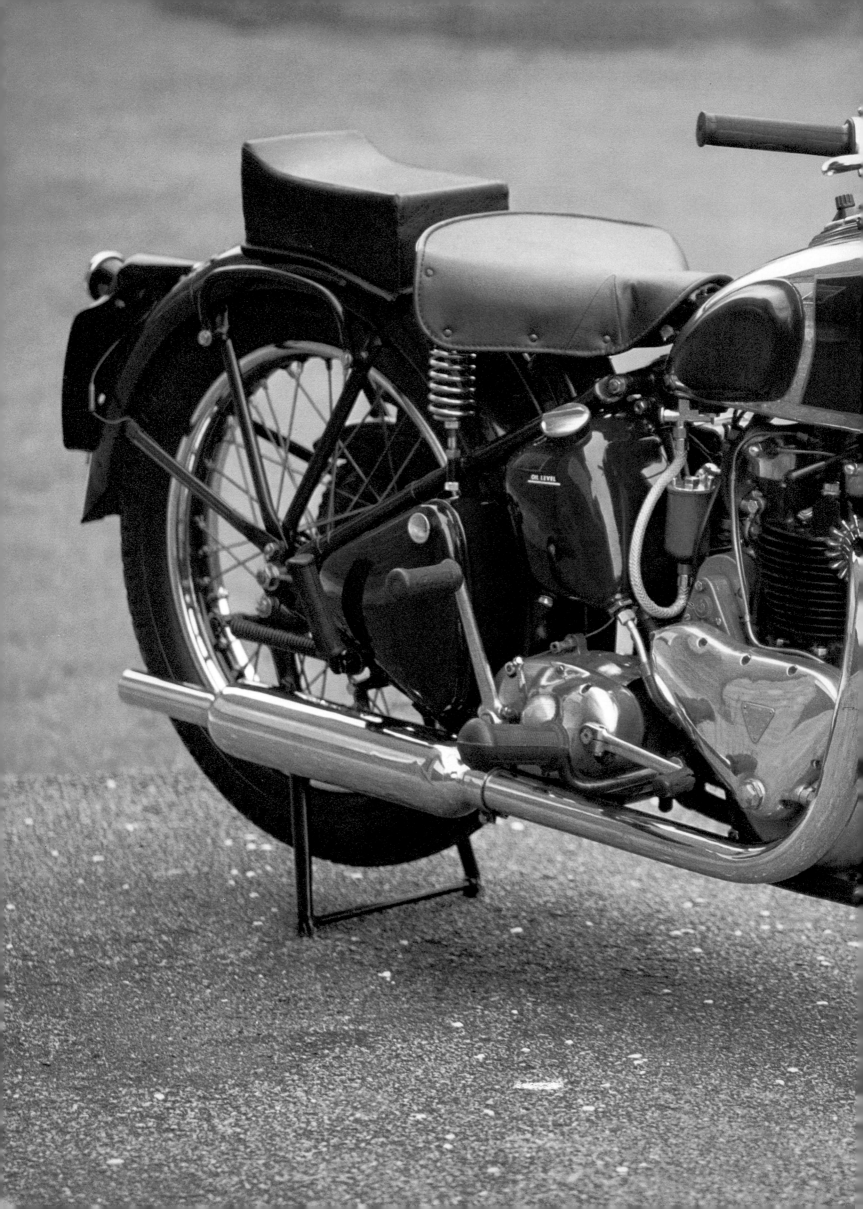

The Rise of the Phoenix: 1940-1955

As the clouds of war threatened the skies of Europe during September 1939, the sporting marques such as Norton, A.J.S., Velocette, B.M.W., Gilera and Moto Guzzi were already heavily involved in building motorcycles which were intended to carry soldiers, airmen and machine guns for the conflict that was to follow. These on-track combatants of a mere few weeks before now found themselves deeply involved in a much more desperate form of confrontation. Motorcycle manufacturers now found themselves part of the great military machines, whether it be to continue making motorcycles or aircraft, armaments and even bombs.

Significantly, the International Six Day Motor Trial (I.S.D.T.) in 1939 was held in swastiked Germany the very week that the Second World War broke out. The competitive specifications required for these off-road machines were in fact just as suited to military use. Thus, not surprisingly, many of the teams entered were also from the military.

The I.S.D.T. was in effect the Olympics of off-road motorcycle sport, but little of the spirit of international friendship was evident that September. Despite assurances of individual safety from the Trials' German military organizers, the British and many other teams surreptitiously on Government advice raced back home mid-trial and overnight to begin the real battle. In war B.M.W. and Zundapp continued to rely on their peacetime-based flat-twin configurations for war work, which even went on to include three wheel and tank track-type rear-end drives. Moto Guzzi and Gilera supplied the more fortunate Italian army riders with truly sporting singles and twins, hardly one step removed from their peacetime counterparts.

Left : The W.D.G3L 350-cc Matchless, which was to the Allies during the Second World War what the 2¾-horsepower Douglas was in the first one.

American Harley-Davidson and Indian machines were sent to beleaguered Britain under the Lend-Lease scheme, to back up the drab khaki-painted Norton 16H and B.S.A. M20 side-valvers, Triumph, Velocette and Royal Enfield O.H.V. 350s and most especially the immortal Matchless G3L.

Neither the war-torn European or American motorcycle factories were particularly concerned with innovation in those dark days. Instead they vied for the only contracts that would keep their industries' wheels turning and that was the mass production of cheap, reliable – but definitely unexciting – motorcycles for military use.

Of the British contingent, only the Matchless could be considered a sporting machine. It was developed from the A.M.C. parent company's peppy pre-war A.J.S. and Matchless trials machines, but with the then-unique-in-Britain, oil-damped telescopic front forks. Small and

Derived from the W.D.G3L, the G3C competition Matchless and its near-identical twin sister, the A.J.S. 16C, dominated the post-war reliability trials scene.

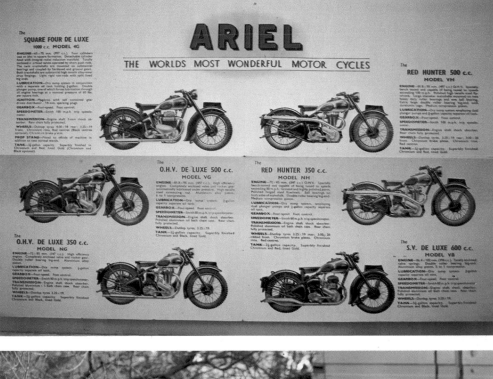

Evidence of the Spartan raw materials of the post-war age, Ariel's 1947 catalogue range.

The A.J.S. 16C trials version of Matchless's competition G3C.

light with an overhead valve, the W.D. G3L was a little cracker. Many ex-racing, scrambling or trials men, now obliged to wear military uniforms, lost little time in tuning their machines further, so that, quite contrary to the military intent, these machines were surreptitiously engaged in spontaneous sporting contests throughout the Second World War.

The end of hostilities brought Britain petrol shortages and rationing along with a chronic lack of raw materials. Everything – steel, aluminium, chromium and rubber, the very ingredients of motorcycle manufacture – was now more urgently required to rebuild shattered cities than wheeled transport. Financially, because of the wartime Government contracts, the motorcycle factories were, ironically, healthier than ever before, but were totally frustrated by their inability to purchase the very iron and steel so necessary to meet the clamouring public's peacetime demand for their products.

The German and Italian industries were dismantled by the Allied victors who took the 'proceeds' back to their own countries where materials and petrol for motorcycles were, for a long time, among the lowest items on most Governments' priority list. The law of supply and

Perhaps too radical for its time, Douglas's 350-cc Mk 5 flat-twin roadster was years ahead of its rivals with its torsion-bar front and rear suspension.

demand was held in limbo as the 1940s marched past and the 1950s began. Once again Europe's motorcycle industry was profoundly damaged.

In Britain, however, a 'deal' was struck between the motorcycle factories and the Ministry of Supply in 1947 which allowed limited resumption of motorcycle sport. Special petrol dispensation was awarded to the works test riders, and it was in the field of reliability trials that their glances first turned. Because each of the major factories still had at least one War Department model, a machine which had been specifically designed for rough roads, those were the models chosen as most suitable for modification to peacetime trials testing. (Incidentally, the limitations of the then-enforced 80-octane pool petrol virtually ruled out highly tuned racing engines anyway.)

So began the era of the great British four-stroke trials motorcycle. Matchless's W.D.G3L, repainted black with resplendent silver lining, became the G3C (competition) and its even more famous and near-identical A.J.S. sister, the 16MC (identical except for the tank badges, magneto position and gold instead of silver lining), which in the hands of such riders as Artie Ratcliffe and Hugh Viney, almost made the post-war Scottish Six Day Trials A.M.C.'s own property.

In the eight years from 1947 to 1954, Viney or Ratcliffe on the black-tanked A.J.S. or Matchless product (which were still virtually the rigid-rear-end wartime G3L) won the Scottish six times between them, while Norton's designers, who had used the old-fashioned 500-cc side-valve engines in their own W.D. machines, were obliged to fit their overhead-valve model 18 roadster engine into the higher-ground-clearance W.D. chassis, add teleforks, and re-design the petrol tank to produce the 500T Trials model.

Norton's classic never actually won the Scottish Six Days Trial, but in the hands of such riders as Johnny Draper, Ted Breffitt, and Geoff Duke (later to become many times World Road-racing Champion), it certainly won everything else and, like the A.M.C.s, many are still in use today.

Triumph had been altogether less fortunate. The Coventry plant had received a direct hit from the Luftwaffe during the Blitz which destroyed not just the factory itself, but the tools, jigs and even blue-prints and spares for the company's entire range of single-cylinder machines. It was impossible for Triumph to supply anything even approaching the large numbers of machines that Norton, Matchless or

Left : Douglas's ill-fated competition model was unique in trials, with its rather wide and vulnerable flat-twin engine.

The ultimate development in the art of designing rigid-rear-end trials machines, the 500T model. When photographed, this one had just been restored by the author for modern-day trials usage.

B.S.A. had done so profitably during the war. As if that were not bad enough for the Triumph management and work force at the then-new Meriden Works outside of blitzed Coventry, by the time the team did have a War Department specification machine ready to offer, the war was obviously almost over and the bulk of the expected government contracts failed to appear.

Triumph's W.D. model was called the TRW, and was based on a pre-war Trials Triumph frame but, like A.M.C.s, with oil-damped tele-scopic forks added and an Edward-Turner-designed side-valve twin engine, aimed at producing plenty of bottom-end torque at low revs to suit rough going.

As Triumph's peacetime production tottered back to normality with only a two machine range, Turner's pre-war Speed Twin and Tiger 100, suitably re-vamped, the factory was in a competition quandary: although the surplus W.D. machines would, like Nortons, provide the basic cycle, the side-valve engine was too slow and heavy for either scrambles or road racing.

Triumph's problem was solved by a piece of opportunism of near genius proportions – ex-Brooklands Ace, Freddie Clarke, who happened to work in the Meriden Experimental Department, remembered that the factory had also built a wartime generator engine for the Lancaster bomber (and Lancasters were not being ordered either!).

Because of the aluminium shortage after the war, Triumph's Speed Twins and Tiger 100s sported all cast-iron cylinders and cylinder heads which made them far too heavy for competitive use. The Lancaster's generator engine, of course, was made for the war effort without such restrictions and had the cylinder heads and barrels beautifully cast in ultra-lightweight alloy.

It did not take Clarke long to liberate a pair of surplus components which, as luck would have it, fitted directly onto the roadster Twins engine's bottom end. So fitted, a Triumph Tiger 100 won the very first post-war road race in the Isle of Man, the 1946 Amateur Manx Grand Prix, winning worldwide recognition for the firm.

Naturally enough, Triumph soon stripped out all of the now-surplus Lancaster bomber generator engines and marketed a road-racing replica of the winning machine. It was called appropriately enough, the Grand Prix Model, after its Manx success.

Although popular, the 'Grand Prix' never really lived up to its early promise. Clarke's next move was to use that same wartime engine top half; but this time he fitted it to the untuned Speed Twin engine, and substituted this latest pairing for the side-valve engine in the W.D. TRW, this time for off-road use. He entered it in the first post-war International Six Days Trial, held in 1948. At short notice, Henry Vale, Triumph's specialist competition engine builder, frantically assembled three such-engined machines, following Clarke's Manx Grand Prix idea, for the imminent International to be held in Italy. Incredibly, these veritable 'bitzas' not only won three Gold Medals, but the Team Prize as well, and so aided Britain to win the International Trophy.

Like the Grand Prix before it, the name chose itself. The 'Trophy Triumphs', as the resulting production versions became known,

Triumph's military-mount 500-cc side-valve TRW twin, which itself spawned the exotic I.S.D.T. 'Trophy' model.

In post-war trim, Edward Turner's Speed Twin adopted Triumph's new oil-damped telescopic front forks.

continued in both private and works hands to win everything from road races, International Six Day Gold Medals, Scrambles and One Day Trials, and what was more, they behaved as well on road as on track.

The Trophy could justifiably be claimed to be the original dual-purpose trail bike, pre-empting today's Japanese market monopoly by over 30 years. Its derivatives continued to win for both Triumph and Britain all over the world, including wins on America's flat tracks, until the collapse of the British industry in the 1970s.

Royal Enfield also commenced the post-war trials-machine years with a machine based on their W.D. CO model, but unlike the other factories of the time, this was purely a stop-gap measure. To Royal Enfield must go the credit for bringing competition machine design into the 20th century with its highly specialized purpose-built swinging-arm rear-suspension trials model, introduced as early as 1947.

In those far-off days it was commonly believed that an off-road motorcycle should not have rear springing, the thinking then being that only a rigid frame would keep the rear wheel in sufficient contact with terra firma, and therefore continue to provide traction and forward motion.

Ludicrous as it may now seem with today's 14 inches of rear suspension movement, 1947-motorcycle-design thinking was almost akin to the belief that the world was flat! Thus Enfield's Springer, instead of getting the immediate acclaim its brilliance deserved, was in fact laughed at and even vilified, though the opposition thought nothing of using rear suspension for smooth road racing.

Compare this, the author's 1949 500-cc Norton International Model 30, with its 1937 350-cc counterpart on page 51. Little has changed other than the telescopic front forks.

Justice was at last done when young J. V. (Johnny) Brittain joined the Royal Enfield team and won the 1952 Scottish Six Day Trial to set the trials world alight and force the other manufacturers to at last sit up and take notice of the Enfield's true potential.

Brittain and his rear-sprung Enfield were to win countless national trials, including the British Experts and the Scott Trial several times each, numerous I.S.D.T. Gold Medals and several British Championships, in the days when trials were an entirely British sport, before the rear suspension penny really dropped on the opposition.

On the race tracks the inadequate post-war pool petrol had played havoc with road-racing times and speeds. The low octane rating had even forced the pre-war based machines to be considerably de-tuned, so that whereas, for instance, the 1939 Senior T.T. average race speed had been almost 90 mph, the 1947 event was won at a low 82·81 mph.

By and large the smaller 250-cc, 350-cc or multi-cylinder engines suffered less from pool-petrol problems than the bigger single-cylinder 500s, so that immediately post-war, Velocette's 350-cc KTT was almost unique in taking a Junior T.T. 1-2-3 at speeds actually faster than that company's own 1939 win.

Those works 350-cc Velos in the hands of Freddie Frith and Bob Foster won Grand Prix after Grand Prix all over Europe and thus won the newly approved F.I.M. (Fédération Internationale Motorcycliste) World Championships in both 1949 and 1950, before the factory eventually withdrew from racing because it was just too costly.

The British racing factories had, by and large, benefitted both from the post-war banning of supercharging, although A.J.S. and Velocette had been working on supercharged models before the war, but also from the fact that the once-great Italian and German factories had been banned from competition as punishment for their war efforts.

Norton, again aided by tuning wizard Joe Craig and perhaps even more so by racing's first post-war superstar, rider Geoff Duke, for a while re-assumed its early and mid-1930s supremacy. Duke's Manx model was second to Bob Foster and Velocette in the 1950 World Championships. These Nortons were virtually pre-war machines until the Irish brothers, Rex and Cromie McCandless, invented the revolutionary 'Featherbed' frame. This innovation not only allowed those fortunate Norton works riders to corner faster, but due to the motor-cycle's increased stability, to use more power while doing so.

Duke won both the 1951 350-cc and 500-cc World Championships and repeated the Junior victory in 1952 using virtually the same pre-war designed engine that, prior to the advent of the McCandless miracle, had been too slow. In one year the McCandless brothers' invention and Duke's prowess had increased the T.T. lap speed from 86·93 mph to 92·77 mph.

Just restored, the author's rare 1948 Triumph 'Trophy' is identical to the trio of works machines that won individual Gold Medals and the manufacturer's trophy (from whence their name) in the 1948 to 1952 International Six Days Trials.

Just like before the war, however, it was not long before even the 'Featherbed' was not enough. As soon as the Italian and German companies of Gilera, B.M.W. and N.S.U. with their multi-cylinder machines were re-admitted to motorcycle racing, it was once again only a matter of time before these more advanced engines began to win. After two long years of frighteningly epic races in which the Norton-mounted Duke had been forced to scrap every inch of the way against the faster continentals, the maestro himself succumbed and joined Gilera as its Number One Works Rider for 1953. Norton never again won a World Championship for in Duke, Gilera had the ideal development man.

The old pre-war four-cylinder supercharged Gilera had proved far more adaptable to running with conventional carburettors than either Velocette's 'Roarer' or A.J.S.'s similarly intended supercharged 'Porcupine', so that coupled with Duke's knowledge of frame design and his riding ability, Gilera's handling problems were solved in double quick time.

Initially only built in 500-cc form, the Gilera 4s won the Senior Road-racing World Championship every year but two from 1951 until their withdrawal at the end of 1957. The Gilera 4 engine also formed the basis of the rival Italian M.V. Agusta racer which took over Gilera's mantle, and continued the Italian domination of both 350-cc and 500-cc classes, while ridden by such showmen as John Surtees, Mike Hailwood, Giacomo Agostini and Phil Read, until 1974.

On the roads the era of the parallel twin had begun. It had started back in 1938 with Edward Turner's Triumphs, which were increased in range and size to include such machines as the 650-cc tuned 'Tiger 110', and the trend continued with Bert Hopwood's classic 650-cc B.S.A. Golden Flash and Norton's Dominator Twins.

To road riders at least, it will probably be the B.S.A. 'Golden Flash' for which Hopwood and that entire era will best be remembered. On the

Another machine restored by the author, this Royal Enfield 350-cc Bullet trials model, with its famous number plate 'HNP 331', in the hands of Johnny Brittain won the Scottish Six Days Trial twice and the British Championships, along with countless national and international trials.

Above : With supercharging banned, the pre-war-designed Velocette 350-cc Mk 8 racer enjoyed a new lease of life, to win the 1949 and 1950 Road-racing World Championships.

Left : Like Velocette, Norton too enjoyed a racing reprieve, which saw the Manx model win four more overall world titles before the Italians and then the Japanese took over.

Right : Veteran Arthur Wheeler still races this Italian Moto Guzzi that took him to fourth place in the 1954 250-cc Road-racing World Championships.

Below : Matchless's ill-fated G45 500-cc twin racer, which looked beautiful but with its roadster-based engine lacked both speed and reliability.

one hand big, soft and docile yet on the other deceptively fast (100 mph plus) these machines were virtually without vices, and went on to sell in quite vast numbers worldwide, to enthusiasts, armies, police forces and perhaps most especially, sidecar fanatics, wherever motorcycles were ridden.

The 'Golden Flash' employed the same basic frame as had been used on B.S.A.'s racing single-cylinder 'Gold Star' and, in the early days, even used the same brakes. The combination made the 'Flash' a sure-footed rapid travelling (and stopping) machine that would, via its big lusty 650-cc engine, even out-accelerate B.S.A.'s own smaller 350-cc and 500-cc racers. It handled and stopped better than Turner's Triumphs (and, for that matter, almost every other machine on the road) in its swinging-arm suspension form, and would probably, if still available in today's economy-conscious market, sell in large numbers

Suppressed by the Allied victors, the great Italian Gilera factory was forced immediately after the war to race the relatively simple single-cylinder 'Saturno' model rather than its exotic four.

yet again, had B.S.A. financially been able to weather the later Japanese storm. That, alas, was not to be.

Interestingly, in the early days of the Japanese industry, it was the B.S.A. 'Flash' that they chose to copy, with the Kawasaki aircraft and motorcycle company still offering a near duplicate machine right through to the 1970s. Yet if there was one truly outstanding all round British Competition machine of that era, it had to be B.S.A.'s 'Gold Star' model.

The name came from the pre-war 500-cc B.S.A. Single that, amidst a blaze of publicity, had won a coveted Brooklands Gold Star for bettering the 100 mph lap. Less publicized was the fact that this machine had won those accolades running on dope (high octane methane fuel) rather than petrol, and that its engine bore little internal resemblance to the over-the-counter version.

First produced in 1938 and codenamed the M.24 (it had been developed from the B.S.A. company's roadster 'Empire Star'), the

Right : Typifying the fashions of the 1950s, photographer Nick Nicholls poses on his Ariel twin fitted with an Avon 'Dreamliner' full fairing.

'The world's fastest standard motorcycle' ran the advertising blurb for the 998-cc Vee-twin Vincent. It was also the most expensive, the fact which finally killed it off. This is the 1952 model.

'Goldy', as it affectionately became known, was first re-introduced in post-war form as a 350 cc only, to be formally known as the B.32 Model, 'Gold Star'.

Coincidentally, in 1947 a new T.T. race had been introduced on the Isle of Man, open only to true production machines of which more than 200 examples had to have been built to qualify. This race was to be called the Clubman's T.T. and its intentions were not only to turn back the clock by forbidding the participation of the out-and-out one-off Grand Prix racers that had taken over Europe's racing circuits, but also to offer a cheaper entry into road racing for the new breed of 1940s riders. The race was to continue until 1956.

B.S.A.'s immortal 'Gold Star' won road races, scrambles (motocross) and trials as well as being one of the fastest roadster singles ever built. This is the BB.34 trials version.

Although B.S.A.'s 'Gold Stars' did not in fact win in either 1947 or the following year, by 1949 they had become unbeatable, spurring the factory on to produce a 500-cc version known as the B.34 Model. B.S.A. also produced a range of pistons, cams, wheel sizes and exhaust pipes which could cheaply and simply convert those machines in a matter of a few short hours from out-and-out road racers to tourers, scramblers, or even trials bikes.

From 1949 to 1963 'Gold Stars' won Championships in dozens of different countries in every known branch of motorcycle sport, from North America's flat tracks and Daytona Beach to dozens of Clubman T.T. wins, from Ascot (U.S. Flat Track Championships) or the 1963 Laconia 100 to the Scottish Six Days Trial. They won several British Trials Championships, dozens of International Six Day Trials Gold Medals, American Hillclimbs, and every major scramble of the era.

It is doubtful if any other mass-produced machine in motorcycling's history has ever been quite so successful in so many of the sport's different branches, or so able as an everyday means of transport. Versatility was the password for that well-deserved 'Gold Star' legend in a market, climate and age, the likes of which will probably never be seen again.

Perhaps the greatest machine to die by the end of this era, however, was the 1000-cc Vincent. Although it was never mass-produced, it had taken over where George Brough left off in 1939 to become the world's fastest – and arguably finest quality – motorcycle ever built.

The giant Vee Twins, capable even in roadster form as far back as 1949 of over 125 mph, were innovative to the extreme. The engine itself formed the main frame to which was bolted at one end, modern style cantilever rear suspension and the other, the unique Girdraulic blade front fork. Both front and rear wheels had double brake drums and the wheels themselves could be removed or adjusted in seconds without the need for tools. Sadly, the Vincent's market cost in 1954 had already become appreciably greater than many small cars, so that designer Philip Vincent chose to end production rather than to cheapen the quality of his product.

The Beginning of the End: 1956-1970

In little more than 55 years from the turn of the century, far less than the average human life span, the motorcycle had leapt from the 5-mph horseless carriage creeping along on un-made roads, to the 100-mph commuter bike, or nearer 200-mph racer, travelling on a worldwide network of well-made, metalled roads. Such was progress. Yet much of motorcycling's, like flying's, inherent excitement had also passed; in a nutshell, progress and sophistication had also come to mean mundane.

Perhaps this was the factor that the European and American motorcycle industries overlooked as they happily strove to meet the market demands of the mid-1950s. Perhaps that very rejection of the mundane via exotica has been Japan's success secret.

Every mid-fifties machine was basically well engineered and did its job almost too well, on roads that no longer provided any form of dramatic challenge; the larger and more expensive machines just went and stopped a bit quicker than the smaller and cheaper ones, but inevitably and almost boringly, they all got there just the same.

With so much of the excitement removed, many found that dressing up to ride a motorcycle was tedious and time-consuming. Generations which had grown up, gone to work, and even done their courting aided by a motorcycle – traditionally adding a sidecar to transport their new wives or impending family – now chose the comfort of four wheels rather than two.

Japan has often been blamed for the demise of Europe's motorcycle industry, yet perhaps in truth, Japanese designers alone recognized that excitement was the missing ingredient, and handsomely met the challenge by providing ever-increasing race-style exotica for use by the average rider on the ordinary street.

Norton, A.J.S., Matchless and Velocette had dropped their out-and-out works racing teams by 1955, concentrating instead on competing with over-the-counter models. The production of overhead-camshaft

High in the Scottish Highlands this 1960s competitor struggles up the mountainside whilst competing in the super-tough Scottish Six Days Trial.

Velocettes had already disappeared from the scene along with the all-conquering N.S.U. machines in the lightweight classes. B.M.W. was down to a one-machine solo race effort, although the company still supported sidecar racing, and everyone else competed for second or third place behind the works Moto Guzzis or Gileras.

Both Indians and Vincents had ceased motorcycle production because it was so uneconomical: their prices were already spiralling above those of cheap cars. Yet the giant mass-producing factories such as B.S.A., and to a lesser degree Triumph, were apparently still buoyant.

Amidst the increasing rumblings of forthcoming hard times, it seems odd that the most advanced and exotic motorcycle ever built, was shortly to appear from the tiny and almost non-exporting Italian Moto Guzzi factory on the sleepy shores of Lake Como. Moto Guzzi's fabulous 500-cc double overhead-camshaft Vee formation eight-cylinder racer was designed and built by Ing Carciano and Moto Guzzi's race shop in a few short weeks. Soon after completion it clocked a speed of over 178 mph during the 1957 Belgian Grand Prix at Spa.

Weighing a mere 320 lbs, lighter than the single-cylinder Manx Norton, the Guzzi revved to a fantastic 12,000 rpm from its eight tiny pistons which breathed through eight tiny carburettors and exhaust pipes to churn out over 80 bhp, available at the rear wheel by the end of 1957. Undoubtedly it was the fastest road racer ever built when it was running well, but that unfortunately was not often the case as ignition problems dogged its early race development during that fateful season. At the Isle of Man T.T., for example, Dickie Dale nearly won the Senior, but eventually finished fourth on seven cylinders, having struck trouble en route.

Obvious to all was that it was only a matter of time before the Guzzi became a winner, but unknown to all, time was the one ingredient the V-8 did not have, for although the Italian factory had already agreed terms for Britain's World Champion John Surtees to ride it for the firm

B.S.A.'s ubiquitous two-stroke Bantam, which typified the cheap and cheerful tradition of the British manufacturers whilst providing lacklustre transport for the masses.

Scrambles – thrills and spills in England during the 1950s before the rest of the world took up the sport and rechristened it Motocross.

during 1958, Moto Guzzi had privately been asked, and had reluctantly agreed with all of the other racing factories, to withdraw totally from the sport at the end of 1957.

With costs escalating and prohibitively expensive exotica taking over, the European factories met in secret and sealed a pact to withdraw from racing simultaneously so that no single factory would carry on to reap the winner's publicity and thus sales. To ensure that no one broke this embargo, most immediately even destroyed their historic machines.

M.V. Agusta, who had played second fiddle to Gilera for so long and who was also amongst the signatories, did indeed reappear the following season, much to the other factories' annoyance, to usurp the Moto Guzzi and Gilera mantle. The fire-engine-red M.V.s had the legend 'Privat' written across the streamlining, but that little ploy fooled no one. Meanwhile such machines as the V.8. Guzzis, it was claimed, had been broken up (at least two did survive).

Meanwhile, at least the British four-stroke trials machine, now universally fitted with rear suspension, reached new zeniths in the hands of such new riders as Gordon Jackson and Sammy Miller. Miller was beginning an era in which he was to win over 900 major trials so far and which indeed will surely soon reach the magical total of 1,000. Gordon Jackson, mounted on a special short-stroke A.J.S. back in 1961, won the Scottish Six Days Trial for his fourth time, with an unparalleled mere one penalty mark.

Miller's most famous 500-cc trials Ariel 'G.O.V. 132' now stands honourably retired in pride of place in Britain's National Motor Museum, while the man himself still campaigns and wins on another G.O.V. 132 replica Ariel as his 1,000th win approaches. Unfortunately Ariels, like A.J.S.s and so many others, have long gone out of production.

By 1965 Miller had switched to the Spanish Bultaco firm as Development Rider, to transform the company's previously inept and ugly

The most exotic road-racing machine ever built, Moto Guzzi's eight-cylinder (in banks of four) shaft-drive extravaganza of 1957. Sadly its potential was never to be realized.

duckling first trials machine into an all-dominating secret weapon within weeks. Almost overnight it made the big British trials singles obsolete. Thus began the Spanish two-stroke trials invasion led by Bultaco, and joined by Montesa and Ossa, that is itself reeling today under the joint threats from both Italian and Japanese invasions.

On the downhill road by the late 1950s, already out of touch with their buying public, the British factories were now run mainly by non-riding accountants, rather than those early pioneers who were motivated by love for the machines that they had built. Slowly the British firms slipped into obscurity with their only innovations being more tinsel or chromium plating.

In Germany B.M.W.'s quality motorcycling products had become, like Vincent before them, just too expensive for the market at which they were aimed, and the cycle industry only survived because of B.M.W.'s successful motorcar sales. Zundapp had closed and N.S.U. was swallowed up within the Volkswagen organization where they built motorcars instead.

Norton had been taken over by A.M.C. who also owned most of the lightweight producing factories, but A.M.C., too, was fighting off the attentions of bankruptcy and the official receiver as the new 1960s decade began. The increasing whispers from Japan were still not taken seriously by British industry.

Although Triumph was now owned by B.S.A., and was, in itself, reasonably healthy with new products and a full order book, mostly to North America, Triumph was destined eventually to be all but dragged down by its parent company, but not before Triumph, at one end of the market, announced its new 650-cc 'Bonneville', and, at the other end, the beautiful little four-stroke 'Tiger Cub' or 'Tigress' scooters.

Edward Turner was more than just a shrewd designer; he was also a supreme publicist and a considerably able businessman. One of his

Above right: The new Italian era. Many times World Champion, the British rider John Surtees put the Italian M.V. Agusta machines on the map when he won them their first Senior T.T. in 1956.

Left: John Surtees banks the 500-cc four-cylinder M.V. into the T.T. course's 'Governor's Bridge' hairpin. Surtees went on to become the only man ever to win both the premier motorcycle and the Formula 1 car World Championships.

Left : Almost the last of the once dominant British trials machines, A.M.C. A.J.S. and Matchless 350-cc models pose in ideal surroundings.

wisest decisions was to appoint the Johnson Organization on the American West Coast as the ideal importers for Triumph's products. In fact Johnson was eventually to take most of Triumph's total motor-cycle production.

Johnson had enthusiastically supported the U.S flat track and endurance racing scene with Indians and so, not unnaturally, maintained that same policy as Triumph's U.S. man, including sponsoring such U.S. greats as Bud Elkins and Ted Evans. Ironically in England, Turner himself was against racing.

As the American end of the Triumph operation became increasingly influential, demanding not just more and more, but faster and faster machines, an impasse was almost reached when Turner refused to further stretch or tune his famous Twins, fearing that his design was already at the limit of its development. Despite Turner's feelings, Johnson, however, in 1955 sponsored Texan Johnny Allen on a cigar-shaped streamlined 650-cc Tiger 110 Triumph, for a crack at the still-German-held World Two-wheeled Speed Record on America's Bonne-ville Salt Flats. Allen claimed the record at 214 mph.

Turner the publicist arranged that Allen's machine be shipped to England in time for that year's Motorcycle Show where it took pride of place on the Triumph Stand. Not unnaturally the Americans soon received their super-tuned twin-carburettor machine that they had sought for so long, aptly named the 'Bonneville'. It is still in production today after being taken over by a workers' co-operative.

An Ariel trials 500-cc HT similar to this, the author's restored example, was the last heavyweight machine to win both the Scottish Six Days Trial and the British Trials Champion-ships, back in 1964 in the hands of Sammy Miller.

On the scrambles front B.S.A. and Triumph still battled it out with the big single versus the lighter Triumph Twins, until in 1959 the Birmingham Small Arms factory took a giant step and released its seemingly humble roadster 250-cc C15 which was almost instantly seized, tuned and converted for road racing, scrambling and trials.

Jeff Smith, Brian Martin and Arthur Lampkin took to these little C15s like ducks to water and between them won the Scott and Scottish Trials, countless scrambles and International Six Day Trial Gold Medals, and many other events. But it was in its bored-out form that this unit-construction single was most successful.

Opened out to 340 cc and re-christened the B40, the little C15 became the military machine of the 1960s and early 1970s. As a 440 cc and later full 500 cc it enabled Smith to win the World Motocross Championships twice and thereby achieve immortality for both man and machine.

Harley-Davidson had at last regained some of its sporting image with the famous 55 model CH, 883-cc V-twins, built with all-alloy barrels and cylinder heads along with hydraulic valve operation, to commence the company's 'Sportster' range. Yet surprisingly, Harley-Davidson's racer, the KR model, still retained the old-fashioned side valves. The giant 1215-cc 'Duo Glide' looked after both police and long-distance touring interests, but it was Harley-Davidson's Italian liaison with the Aermacchi factory that set Europe's race tracks alight with super little 250-cc and 350-cc single-cylinder overhead-cam racers that now bore the Harley-Davidson name.

Meanwhile in Japan, Soychiro Honda, who in a Tokyo backstreet had first built a motorized pedal bicycle in 1945, just like the European pioneers of 50 years before, had by 1960 reached the staggering production figure of 168,554 machines a year, to be exported to over 50 countries. Honda had not yet made inroads in Europe's home market, nor was the company regarded as a serious threat. Honda had so far specialized in the production and sale of 250-cc and under, lightweight machines which were mainly exported to the Third World. Foolishly the West thought that these machines would be unlikely to challenge the

By 1965 the magnificent Miller had switched to the Spanish Bultaco lightweight two-stroke machines, to continue winning until today he nears his 1,000th trials victory.

Right : End of the line. Three B.S.A. production racing 'Gold Stars' that were too successful and killed the goose that laid the golden egg. These machines won with such monotony that their racing class itself died, killed off by boredom.

Triumph's unit-construction 'Bonneville', suitably customized for the States.

more macho 650-cc Superbikes of Britain or Germany, yet the writing was on the wall, for in practice those early Japanese 250s found eager buyers largely due to their use of racing technology.

Honda's engines and, perhaps just as important, brakes, were of Grand Prix standards and the resulting machines, though smaller, were often quicker than many of Europe's efforts of twice the little Honda's engine capacity and physical size. Thus the 246-cc o.h.c. 'Dream' and the 125-cc o.h.c. 'Benly' were snapped up by eager buyers when first offered to Europe and are now justifiably deserving of classic status.

Before long there would be a 444-cc parallel-twin Honda, christened the 'Black Bomber' and aimed directly at the markets of such firms as B.S.A. or Triumph. It incorporated such advanced specifications for roadsters as overhead-cam engines and twin leading shoe brakes that neither of the British factories nor B.M.W. could match. Thus the A.M.C. Group of A.J.S., Matchless and Norton finally went under in

the relentless and unequal struggle. The Norton name was later revived, and before the sad end, both B.S.A. and Triumph were, at least temporarily, to answer the Japanese thrust and enjoy more than a few last moments of glory with the Trident Triples that electrified the Isle of Man T.T. and Daytona and became almost the standard racing motorcycle in both Britain and North America.

The Triumph 650-cc Bonneville Twin, which had first been introduced as a highly tuned motorcycle back in 1959, had undergone major re-designs to contain its performance, and it had become obvious that although the United States still demanded an even higher state of tune, the 'Bonny' was now perilously near its limit.

One faction of the Triumph design team suggested merely boring out the 'Bonneville' a full 100 cc to increase its capacity to 750 cc. But Bert Hopwood, by then Deputy Managing Director at Meriden, was convinced that such a course would further unbalance this engine which already had an existing vibration problem (he was later proved correct), and so suggested instead adding a third cylinder.

Intended only as a temporary solution while an entirely new engine was being designed, these Triumph and B.S.A. triples were merely a 'Bonneville' plus one extra cylinder and, in one sense at least, were initially too successful for their own and their maker's good. Born of

Left: Norton's famous 600-cc 'Dominator' twin, race-bred and with superb handling due to its 'Featherbed' frame, became the Cafe racer of the Fifties and Sixties.

Britain's final big-bike racing fling, the G50 500-cc Matchless single, was a bigger version of the equally successful 350-cc A.J.S. 7R.

Left : Last of the traditional B.S.A. sporting twins, the 650-cc 'Rocket Gold Star' was the ultimate version of the famous 'Gold Flash'.

The 'Thruxton' model 500-cc Velocette, so named after it won the Thruxton 500-mile race, took over the production racing mantle of B.S.A.'s by then defunct 'Gold Star'. As a roadster, however, this model was ill suited to road use.

The end was soon to come for the roadster Triples too whose production ceased soon after the Meriden sit-in. B.S.A.'s original road-racing single-cylinder Gold Star had been discontinued several years before, to be replaced for a short period by the Rocket Gold Star, a hybrid made up from a tuned Gold Flash engine placed into a Clubman's racing Gold Star chassis. It was manufactured in small numbers until 1963.

Meanwhile, the once-great-but-tiny racing company of Velocette was now producing only roadsters and struggling against financial disaster after disaster. Several of the company's forward-thinking lightweights had failed to rouse public interest and had failed in the marketplace but Velocette was to produce one last classic racing winner.

The demise of B.S.A.'s single-cylinder Gold Star production racer had created a void and there were very few machines ready or able to fill the tragic gap in both the 500-cc Clubmen's racing and the posers Cafe racing market. Velocette shrewdly decided to re-tune its roadster 'Venom' model.

Most of the work involved re-designing the cylinder and valves of this pushrod-powered engine to enlarge the inlet ports to allow for the use of valves almost as big as proverbial dinner plates. Good carburetion was provided by a giant Amal Grand Prix carburettor; racing clip-on handlebars and rear-set footrests completed the ensemble. So tuned, the Velo won both the Thruxton 500-mile Race and the Production T.T. It sold in relatively large numbers, even for road use, but unfortunately, due to its highly tuned state, it also gained a somewhat deserved reputation as a difficult-to-start, inflexible machine, most suited to the track. Named the 'Thruxton' after its first major success, this 500-cc classic was Velocette's swansong, for it, like so many others, became too expensive to produce economically. Thus Velocette, along with Royal Enfield who shared the manufacturing rights, went quietly out of business.

Though still specializing in smaller machines, Honda, Suzuki and Yamaha between them had taken the world's race tracks apart. With the exotic Honda Twin, four- and six-cylinder four-strokes, and two- and four-cylinder two-strokes, the Japanese dominated all classes from 50 cc to 350 cc. A lone 'outsider', the Italian M.V. concern grimly fought to cling on to the 500-cc crown, despite Mike Hailwood's efforts on a Honda.

Japanese machines, from their first full World Championship Road-racing season in 1961, won almost every race: seven 50-cc World Championship titles, ten 125-cc, nine 250-cc and six 350-cc World titles by the end of 1970. But it was to take millions of yen and five more years before the long-coveted Blue Riband 500-cc Title was also seemingly to become 'permanently' theirs.

The era had begun with Britain almost singlehandedly supplying the majority of the world's motorcycles and had ended with near extinction for the U.K. motorcycle factories. Despite this near-annihilation by the Japanese, Bert Hopwood's original Norton Dominator was temporarily raised from the dead, to be bored out and renamed the 'Commando'.

In truth, only the engine was Hopwood's and by 1967 when the 'Commando' was devised, 20 years after Hopwood's original design, it could hardly still have been considered innovative. Rather it was the frame of the 'Commando' that would go down in history as unique.

Like Triumph and the Triple, the resurrected Norton concern knew that it really needed new mechanical blood, yet the company had little time or money with which to complete a total re-design. Where

Giacomo Agostini guns the final three-cylinder racing M.V. Agusta out of the T.T. course's Bray Hill Dip. Soon that machine too would be overshadowed by the Rising Sun.

Ralph Bryans streaks off on the tiny and all-conquering racing 250-cc Honda 4 to commence his lap of the Isle of Man T.T. course.

Triumph's answer had been to add an additional cylinder because further tuning or boring of the existing engine would have caused vibration problems, Norton too adopted a novel answer. Doctor Steven Bauer, a nuclear physicist, had somewhat oddly joined the new Norton/Villiers Company as Director of Engineering and had come up with a totally different answer. (Lest it be thought that Dr. Bauer, who had never ridden a motorcycle in his life, was an ill-conceived choice, he was at least able to dispense with traditional, and perhaps more to the point, pre-conceived ideas.) For the 'Commando', Bauer and his team decided to let the big engine continue to vibrate and indeed, eventually to bore it out to a full 850 cc from its original 500-cc concept. *But* to alleviate the

The late great S.M.B. (Mike) Hailwood on his way to yet another World Championship win on the fabulous-sounding but evil-handling Honda 6.

vibration problem they chose to mount the entire engine, gearbox and rear-wheel-carrying swinging arm on isolastic rubber suspension blocks. This meant that the engine and entire transmission could happily shake and shudder away, completely isolated from the rest of the machine and its rider. The idea was to prove an unparalleled success; the 'Commando' sold worldwide to a vast market as anything from a police machine, a roadster, even to a racer.

At the time of Norton's final demise, the engine that should have taken the firm into the 1980s with radical engineering design and principles, had been commissioned and constructed from the Cosworth Racing-car Engine Company, and it had even raced in prototype form under the name 'Norton Challenge'. But sadly the financial sands of time had run out on this once great company that had graced the world's race tracks in an unbroken run from 1907 until 1975.

Left : Perhaps one of the ugliest motorcycles ever built, the 'Münch Mammut', with its enormous N.S.U. car engine protruding either side.

Above : Looking slightly more conventional, this example of the Münch Mammut was shipped to America for an attempt on the world two-wheeled speed record. It failed and its manufacturers went bankrupt soon after.

Left : Norton superbike of the Seventies, the 850-cc 'Commando', with its rubber bush-mounted engine. On the left is the John Player racer replica, on the right the standard production roadster.

99

Age of the Superbike: 1970 Onwards

The very word 'superbike', applied to motorcycles, is a descriptive misnomer which today tends merely to imply large capacity motorcycles capable of particularly high speeds, rather than perhaps the original usage which was intended to describe machines that (by the 1970s) had reached a previously undreamed of degree of sophistication and general excellence, regardless of capacity.

Motorcycles today, as almost the general rule, will, from 250 ccs upwards, out-accelerate any car, have disc brakes capable of bringing the machine to an almost instant halt, have electric starters to remove the age-old chore of kick starting, and even have flashing turn indicators.

Tested on the race tracks tyres too have improved immeasurably to allow new freedoms to both machine designer and rider. Thus despite the modern machines' quite vast increases in power over their predecessors of a mere decade ago on an equal capacity basis, the motorcycles of today are capable of being faster yet safer than ever before.

The Japanese invasion, which in the bigger classes had been blunted by their initial inability to make either their chassis or tyres capable of safely containing the general excellence, or perhaps more to the point, speed potential, of their engines, at least forced Europe's remaining designers to re-think the entire concept of their own offerings.

'Joe Public' undoubtedly gained as manufacturer after manufacturer, faced with Japan's challenge, was at long last forced to re-think its own products, correct obvious deficiencies, and offer more to the new all-powerful buyer for little or no extra money. Interestingly the re-thinks resulted in a enormous choice of machines for the buying public from the devastatingly simple to the frighteningly exotic: on the one hand, the owner, in true motorcycling tradition, could still do his or her own maintenance or, on the other hand, he could possess a bike which was so complex that only a highly trained specialist and costly dealer service would suffice.

By no means did all of the complex designs originate in Japan. M.V. Agusta, although no longer racing by then, opened out the engine of its 500-cc four-cylinder racer to 750 cc, added shaft drive and sold the resulting machine at considerable cost to those few wealthy fans of these Italian products who could afford them. Also in Italy, Benelli produced a six-cylinder across-the-frame-engined machine of 750-cc capacity that looked suspiciously like a 500-cc Honda 4 with an additional two extra cylinders. But by and large Italy, Germany and Britain were, with the exception of Triumph's Trident, to stick with big, lusty, powerful but simple engines.

Triumph's re-designed Trident, re-christened the T160 and with an electric starter, now had most of its earlier design faults ironed out as a result of Doug Hele's undoubted genius coupled with practical experience gained from the race machines.

Norton, likewise, took a fresh look at its 'Commando' and produced a full 850-cc version in both electric- and kick-start form. Norton also produced a successful replica of its John Player sponsored racer with full track-type streamlining and colours. B.M.W., on the other hand, was forced to drop its beautifully engineered, but by then too heavy, expensive and slow, R50 and R60 models and completely re-design.

Spirit of today – typical U.S. individualism expressed on the mundane and mass-produced Japanese 4.

In Italy the famous Ducati concern of Bologna introduced the beautiful in-line 750-cc Vee Twins in touring, sporting and racing form, while, similarly, Moto Guzzi built the 'Le Mans' production racer/roadster, initially as a 750 cc and later as a 850 cc, with its Vee engine set across the frame and coupled to the rear wheel via shaft drive.

Whichever machine or factory was involved, North America was the common denominator. In Europe the whole market had changed – the commuter was no longer necessarily a motorcycling enthusiast, but was, instead, a purchaser of by-and-large the smallest, cheapest and most economical machine of any range. The manufacturer of the more profitable superbike just did not fit into this picture!

In truth, the late 1970s and early 1980s from the production and sales points of view have really been the age of the moped (light motorcycle of 50 cc or less with pedals attached). A steadily diminishing number of enthusiasts have bought superbikes because they want something more than just a source of transport. For them the motorcycle was and is a provider of excitement which holds a joy of possession that their cars can never offer.

Only in affluent North America, and even there most especially in the warmer States such as California, could the manufacturer find the sort of eager market that had once been Europe itself back in the 1950s, a market which included machines of all shapes and sizes required to satiate a new demand of near-cult proportions.

Europe itself could no longer support its own motorcycle industry which was now so heavily dependent on large capacity machines and the U.S. export market, and it was that very weakness which forced even more of Europe's own companies into bankruptcy when the U.S. Government announced the new rigid exhaust emission laws.

Just as the arrival of the supercharger had caused chaos during the 1930s, these new laws issued Norton, Moto Guzzi, B.M.W., Ducati and Triumph's Bonneville and others with a challenge they could hardly meet, for each of those machines relied on highly tuned, large-capacity twin-cylinder engines for their excellent performance.

Left: Grace and speed were implied by the inclusion of the speedboat in this picture of the late-Seventies F.I. 750-cc Honda supersports 4.

Yet another manifestation of the owner's individuality, where almost 1,000 lights and acres of chromium plate transform this standard Harley-Davidson into a unique, though rather heavy, example.

Overleaf: In an age of increasing mechanical complexity Jerry Dean amply demonstrates that there is still room for the simple engineering and fine handling of this Italian Ducati during the 1982 Daytona Speed Week.

Lead-free gasoline and silencing restrictions meant that those manufacturers had to de-tune their products completely which, in turn, meant that exciting sportsters were transformed almost overnight into docile tourers in Harley-Davidson's own image, and thus lost the very performance figures and appeal that had sold them in the first place.

Japan's Honda concern, like Gilera in the 1930s, had placed its trust in complex four-cylinder engines in whose tiny cylinders the fuel octane was infinitely less important. But perhaps wisest of all, Honda's vast moped sales throughout the world were profitable enough to enable the company to withstand the necessary vast development costs of designing afresh for the United States.

Honda, who had always pinned its future on four-stroke engines, staked its successful claim at that time to over 50 per cent of the world's motorcycle market. Other Japanese manufacturers such as Kawasaki, Suzuki and Yamaha, who had favoured two-stroke machines, were hit almost as hard by the new American laws as any of the European makes. The two-stroke motorcycle burned a mixture of petrol and oil which led to severe exhaust emission and pollution problems. Although their racers and off-road machines stayed true to the two-stroke cause, these other Japanese firms were forced to develop, somewhat frantically, four-stroke road machines for that all-important U.S. road-riding dollar market.

Kawasaki's 750-cc H2 three-cylinder two-stroke, affectionately known as the 'Mach 3', and most definitely not suitable for the U.S.'s tough emission laws, had first appeared in Europe in 1969 where it won a wholly justified reputation as the most frightening, fastest, and evil-looking motorcycle ever to leave Japan; yet ironically, it was almost

Right: America's 1982 World 500-cc Motocross Champion, Brad Lackey, who has ridden for most of the major Japanese factories, seen here on the big Kawasaki.

Below left: The American Team B.M.W.s at Laguna Seca, where these Teutonic twins in the hands of such U.S. stars as Ron Pierce, John Long and Kurt Liebmann kept winning long after their time.

Below: Erik Gundersen of Denmark and Bobby Schwarz of the U.S.A. battle it out in front during the 1982 World Team Speedway Final which was won by America.

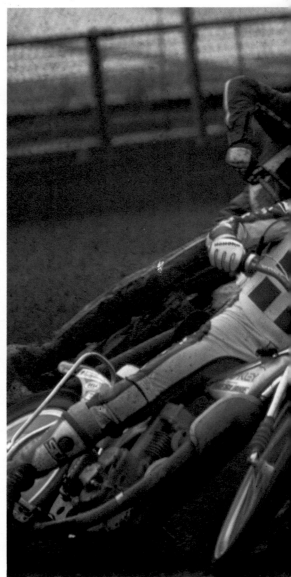

Left : Now one of
the world's fastest
growing sports,
schoolboy
motocross. These
youngsters are off
on the massed
start at a U.S.
race meeting.

worshipped by its owners. This was the original wheelie machine. Built
at a time when neither Japanese tyres nor frames were particularly well
developed, the Kawasaki's extreme power could be near lethal and gave
away nothing to commonsense or economy, guzzling fuel at less than 20
miles to the gallon as its front wheel pawed the air at the slightest whiff
of the throttle from its 74 bhp engine. It was not its top speed that made
this machine stand out from the pack, but rather the rate at which it got
there, for this was a he-man's motorcycle that produced more adrenalin
more often in the blood (often due to its poor handling) than any other
motorcycle of the day ever could. One is almost reminded again of that
long-lost pioneer spirit of motorcycling.

Kawasaki was again to produce such an animal with its four-cylinder
900-cc Z1 four-stroke machine, when forced by U.S. law eventually to
abandon its two-stroke roadster development; this time the new
machine was known as the Z900, but it possessed only marginally better
handling than its predecessor. The raw, powerful, double-overhead-
cam design Z900 engine was – and is – arguably the best power unit ever
to leave Japan and when shod with superior European tyres, its
handling improves immeasurably. Z900s have already become
collector's items today. The original Z900 engines reaped many racing
successes and formed the basis of every single subsequent Kawasaki
four-stroke engine.

Since those days, Kawasaki engines have become the ones by which
all others tend to be judged. Fortunately their chassis have improved

An image machine
par excellence,
*Harley-
Davidson's
'Sportster',
photographed on
the streets of San
Francisco.*

109

Reaching for the sky, this U.S. motocross ace amply demonstrates the skills needed in the growing sport of artificial-circuit stadium motocross racing, originated in America and now sweeping Europe.

quite dramatically, forcing the motorcycles to renounce their once-justified reputation for dramatic handling. The improvements were an advancement undoubtedly aided and abetted by a successful race team effort in both Europe and North America.

Such riders as Eddie Lawson on Kawasaki 'Green Meanies' won the U.S. Superbike Championships in both 1981 and 1982, and Kork Ballington and Anton Mang between them have won every 250-cc or 350-cc road-racing World Championship title but two, since 1979.

Ironically, although Honda was now the world's greatest and most profitable motorcycle-producing company, and had, in the late 1960s and early 1970s, poured vast fortunes into the quest for the World 500-cc Road-racing Championship, it was to be the smaller Yamaha concern that was to eventually break M.V.'s domination.

Taking a page from Gilera's 1953 book, when the Italian company bought rival Norton star, Geoff Duke, to win for them, Yamaha similarly, in 1975, tempted Italian multi-world M.V. Agusta champion, Giacomo Agostini, to spearhead its effort to become the first to win the 500-cc World Crown with a Japanese machine.

Fourth during that 1975 500-cc title hunt was the Finn, Tepi Lansivouri, on a Suzuki, a machine that, at that time, was hardly a force to be

Right: The original Kawasaki Z900 machines, prepared in anger for American streetbike racing.

reckoned with, but a year later in the hands of Britain's Barry Sheene, Suzukis, rather than Yamahas or M.V.s, became the machines to beat. With the sole exceptions of American Kenny Roberts' wins in 1977/78/79, Hamamatsu-built Suzukis have won the World 500-cc Crown ever since.

Like Kawasaki, the Suzuki Company, prior to the U.S.A.'s stringent emission laws, had put its roadster faith in two strokes, but unlike Kawasaki had relied mainly on big 750-cc water-, rather than air-cooled, engines, which, though not quite as quick, were much more efficient in terms of petrol economy. But it was as producers of the revolutionary Wankel rotary-engined R.E.5 that Suzuki's mid-1970s era will perhaps best be remembered.

The R.E.5 was to Japan what the Ariel 'Pixie', B.S.A. 'Dandy' and Velocette 'Viceroy' had been to Britain. In short, it was a hopelessly expensive disaster. Once again a major motorcycle manufacturer had totally misread the interests of the buying public, a costly error which almost caused Suzuki's termination.

Left : Belgian trials star Eddie Lejune gave the Japanese giants Honda their first World Trials Championship title win. He is seen here competing in an arena trial.

Britain's Rob Shepherd competing on the works Honda in the Scottish Six Days Trial before going on to win the British Championships.

Right : Suzuki's R.E.5 Wankel, the development of which cost the Hamamatsu company so dearly.

Below : America's brilliant first 500-cc Road-racing World Champion Kenny Roberts pilots his four-cylinder two-stroke Yamaha at nearly 200 mph around Daytona's banking.

Left : Phil Read waits on the start grid with his 500-cc racing M.V. Agusta, by then already outclassed by the Japanese two-stroke invasion.

Hailed initially as a revolution by its original European investors, the well-patented Wankel idea promised to be the internal combustion engine of the future. Suzuki and others rushed in to pay vast sums to acquire the licensing rights in an ill-fated quest to be the first to perfect and market tomorrow's machine.

In fairness, the resulting Suzuki motorcycle was quite brilliant in concept and design, silky smooth and quick on the road, although far too thirsty on petrol and at 560 lb, much too heavy ever to be considered a sporting motorcycle. However, regardless of its innovative genius, in practice it did little – if anything – better than a conventional machine and the buying public just did not want to know.

Honda, who by then had the most comprehensive range of machines, engine configurations and capacities ever seen in motorcycling's history, had also got a problem with a rather too heavy and underpowered, though beautifully engineered, 350-cc four-cylinder machine that, despite vast development costs, like Suzuki's R.E.5, the customers did not want.

In a simple stroke of genius, the parent factory acknowledged that it would probably never sell in the United States, the country for which it

Overleaf : Virginio Ferrari of Italy on the works 500-cc Suzuki leads similarly mounted team-mate Randy Mamola (U.S.A.), 1981 World Champion Marco Lucchinelli and his Honda, Jack Middleburg and Guido Paci during the 1982 San Marino Grand Prix.

had been originally designed, so Honda bored out the engine to a larger 400 cc and re-vamped the cycle side to look like a European racer. Honda correctly reasoned that the surplus units might then sell in Europe.

Those tiny 1975 and onwards 400-cc four-cylinder air-cooled C.B.400F supersports machines were in a very real sense Japan's first lesson in constructing a machine especially for European, rather than American tastes, and from the word 'go' the grateful European public acknowledged the bike a winner. It sold in vast numbers to commuter and sporting riders alike, and went on to win T.T.s and Formula World Championship Road races.

Uncharacteristically, for a period of time in the mid- to late 1970s, the entire Japanese industry misread market trends and instead of capitalizing on designs such as that of the little Honda, embarked on an era of mammoth machines of up to 1300-cc capacity which displayed a degree of speed and performance no road rider could adequately use.

Yamaha, Kawasaki and Honda spent fortunes developing machines like the 1100-cc Honda Gold Wing which sold in North America but flopped in Europe, the Z1300 Kawasaki, the six-cylinder 1100-cc C.B.X., and so on. Suzuki, on the other hand, probably wiser after its disastrous R.E.5 experience, was alone in settling for the much more commonsense and sporting G.S.1000 to the eternal gratitude of a reviving European industry.

Norton and M.V. had both of them gone to the wall already but B.M.W., Moto Guzzi, Laverda and Ducati had steadily trimmed their operations to concentrate on building machines more suited to European roads. They became specialists in producing high quality race-proven designs where, instead of speed being the ultimate criteria, it was superb handling. They produced large-capacity motorcycles which were fast enough, yet not too heavy.

Honda's fabulous little 400-cc four-cylinder C.B.400F, the Japanese machine designed for Europe, to win in the marketplace and on track.

Right : Honda's mighty C.B.X. six-cylinder 1100-cc roadster was almost a direct uprate of Mike Hailwood's 500-cc Grand Prix road racer of the 1960s. Unfortunately the giant machine was just too big, fast, heavy and complex to sell in large numbers.

With the ultra-heavy mammoth Japanese superbikes falling on hard times, even the U.S. motorcyclists once more looked to European manufacturers. At last the world's great marketplaces began again to distinguish between the necessary compromises: on the one hand, the street racer, and on the other, the tourer.

B.M.W.'s streamlined 1000-cc twin-cylinder R100S, with its feather-bed Norton-devised frame and all-up weight of little more than 400 lb (one-third less weight than any Japanese equivalent), led the new European onslaught bought, as it was, by discerning riders who knew that ultimate speed was only part of motorcycling's promise.

Similarly, B.M.W.'s 750-cc and later 850-cc 'Boxer Twins' gained a healthy slice of the American market as machines that might not do much more than 110 mph, but would do so indefinitely without fuss or strain due to their lightweight and simple design, and that their owners could successfully maintain themselves.

Left: Britain's Barry Sheene contesting the 1982 Spanish Grand Prix on his Yamaha before his horrendous crash later in the season.

Expensive, but smooth, comfortable, reliable and practical, B.M.W.s lead the European motor-cycle market revival with machines like this 800-cc R80RT.

Moto Guzzi replied with its T.3 and later 'Spada' shaft-drive models, each very much in the B.M.W. mould. Perhaps most important was the fact that all of these machines could be stripped and if necessary re-built, right by the roadside. The mechanics of a Japanese bike were, by this time, beyond the skills of all but a trained mechanic.

Ducati concentrated instead on following the ultra-lightweight formula, but in superb sports form, with large-capacity outright racing engines and advanced desmodromic valve gear. These machines have been (and are) raced very successfully by such riders as Freddie Spencer (now with Honda) and Jim Adamo on American race tracks, and by the late great Mike Hailwood, who beat the might of Honda in the Isle of Man T.T.

For a time as the 1970s came to a close, Moto Guzzi's tuned 'Le Mans' model, Ducati's 900s and even B.M.W.s won again on both American and European race tracks. But such successes were doomed

Overleaf: The young pretender Randy Mamola shows triple World Champion and fellow American Kenny Roberts the way round during the Dutch T.T. in this Suzuki versus Yamaha battle.

The 1982 World 500-cc Road-racing Champion Franco Uncini on his Suzuki looks pensive as he waits on the line to commence the race.

Right: Tomorrow's star today – the brilliant young American road racer Freddie Spencer on his works N.S. three-cylinder Honda. In his and Honda's World-Championship two-stroke debut year the pairing finished third overall in the Blue Riband 500-cc class.

not to last long, however, as Japan at last learned the lesson of its own C.B.400F Honda, and once again turned the corner.

After a long absence, Honda itself turned envious glances back towards the World Championship race tracks: 500-cc Grand Prix road racing, U.S. Flat Tracks, World Motocross honours, and even trials. The big 'H' soon made fresh efforts as part of its quest to maintain its giant market share via race-track-winning publicity.

The world's motocross circuits were soon to reverberate to a most uncharacteristic Honda sound as the four-stroke manufacturer adopted the two-stroke formula for both scrambling and Enduros to win the World Championships with such riders as Britain's Graham Noyce and Belgium's Andre Malherbe. For road racing and trials Honda continued to put its faith in the four stroke. Honda's top secret (at the time) N.R.500 Vee four-cylinder Grand Prix racer, with its oval cylinders and ceramic pistons, 18 valves all bolted into a pressed aluminium chassis, and tiny wheels with giant section tyres, went from being a predicted world beater to becoming the most expensive flop in racing history. It failed even to qualify on each of its early outings against the opposition two-strokes.

Suzuki's and Yamaha's square-four two-stroke racers continued to look unthreatened by Honda's 'megabuck' efforts throughout the 1977

to 1981 period, until the Honda company gave in and announced that it too was throwing in the towel to build a racing two-stroke, to be known as the N.S.500 and to be loosely based on the company's world-beating scramblers.

The young American Ace, Freddie Spencer, in conjunction with the Italian World Champion, Marco Lucchinelli, and the Japanese rider, Takazumi Katayama, affectionately known as the Flying Taxi, gave these new Hondas fairytale 1982 debuts with numerous fastest laps and several wins in the 500-cc World Championships. The success story could well have given Freddie Spencer second place overall to the little Italian Franco Uncini's Suzuki had Spencer not crashed when in the lead during the German Grand Prix, the final race of the season.

Right: Kawasaki's G.P.Z.550, with its race-bred Unitrac rear suspension and 130-mph potential, hailed the beginnings of a new, lighter, and more common-sense aproach from Japan.

Voted 1982 Machine of the Year in Britain, the 550-cc Honda C.B.X., like Kawasaki's similar-sized G.P.Z., demonstrates Japan's new dawning with common-sense, relatively lightweight machines.

As Honda now also threatened to win the 500-cc World Road-racing Championships, the only class it has never won, both the Japanese and European industries have embarked on a more commonsense approach to the roadster market in the 1980s.

Following on, though somewhat belatedly, in the 400-cc Honda 4's footsteps, has come the C.B.X. 550, a small light machine in the true European mould, capable of a staggering 130 mph. Similarly Kawasaki has scaled down its 1100-cc superbike, added monoshock race suspension, and likewise produced a supersporting 130 mph roadster called the G.P.Z.550.

Suzuki, with its 'Katana' range, and Yamaha, with its 'Seca' (named after the U.S. race track), have been somewhat less successful as Honda and Kawasaki race ahead in the marketplace. But the fabulous little Yamaha R.D.350 LC two-stroke twins, developed straight from Yamaha's on-track racers, had helped to turn the motorcycling wheel the full circle.

Right: Britain's ill-fated Hesketh, the Rolls-Royce elect of motor-cycling, got off to a sad start when the company went into liquidation in 1982. However, there is still hope that the Hesketh will yet be saved.

The future, or yet another Japanese wrong turning? This ultra-modern-looking X.J.650 Yamaha is one of a new breed of highly complex machines fitted with on-board computer and turbo-charging.

In Britain, Lord Hesketh introduced his super quality, ultra-expensive Vee Twin in an attempt to follow Vincent and Brough's policy of decades before, only to end, like Hesketh's predecessors, in financial disaster. But Triumph could yet bounce back with its 1982 Daytona-winning eight-valve 750-cc T.S.S. However, even as the European products struggle to retain a place in the market, Japan is already turning a new corner.

Complex turbo-charging and/or petrol injection, even on-board computers, are now featured by every one of the Japanese makes on at least one model of their range for 1983 – once again, of course, user self-maintenance is virtually impossible.

Whether these innovations will become, like Suzuki's R.E.5, marketing mistakes, or are the pointers for the future, it is too early to tell, but tomorrow's motorcycle mechanic is already becoming a space age technician, and the products a far cry from a mere decade ago.